Options for Strengthening ROK Nuclear Assurance

BRUCE W. BENNETT, KANG CHOI, CORTEZ A. COOPER III,
BRUCE E. BECHTOL, JR., MYONG-HYUN GO,
GREGORY S. JONES, DU-HYEOGN CHA, UK YANG

 NATIONAL SECURITY RESEARCH DIVISION

 THE ASAN INSTITUTE for POLICY STUDIES

For more information on this publication, visit **www.rand.org/t/RRA2612-1**.

About RAND

The RAND Corporation is a research organization that develops solutions to public policy challenges to help make communities throughout the world safer and more secure, healthier and more prosperous. RAND is nonprofit, nonpartisan, and committed to the public interest. To learn more about RAND, visit www.rand.org.

Research Integrity

Our mission to help improve policy and decisionmaking through research and analysis is enabled through our core values of quality and objectivity and our unwavering commitment to the highest level of integrity and ethical behavior. To help ensure our research and analysis are rigorous, objective, and nonpartisan, we subject our research publications to a robust and exacting quality-assurance process; avoid both the appearance and reality of financial and other conflicts of interest through staff training, project screening, and a policy of mandatory disclosure; and pursue transparency in our research engagements through our commitment to the open publication of our research findings and recommendations, disclosure of the source of funding of published research, and policies to ensure intellectual independence. For more information, visit www.rand.org/about/principles.

RAND's publications do not necessarily reflect the opinions of its research clients and sponsors.

Published by the RAND Corporation, Santa Monica, Calif.
© 2023 RAND Corporation
RAND® is a registered trademark.

Library of Congress Cataloging-in-Publication Data is available for this publication.

ISBN: 978-1-9774-1214-0

Cover: U.S. Army photo by Staff Sgt. Ken Scar.

About This Report

In this report, we describe a combined research effort between the RAND Corporation and the Asan Institute for Policy Studies that focused on options for strengthening Korean assurance of the U.S. nuclear umbrella offered to the Republic of Korea (ROK). It is a follow-on to a paper on the North Korean nuclear weapon threat issued in 2021 (Bennett et al., 2021) and a report on North Korean chemical and biological weapons, electromagnetic pulse, and cyber threats issued in 2022 (Bennett et al., 2022). As the North Korean nuclear weapon threat has grown, there has been considerable ROK interest in building an independent ROK nuclear weapon force. However, doing so could become a major disaster for the ROK and the United States. In this report, we suggest options that could be taken by the ROK and U.S. governments to strengthen ROK nuclear assurance of the U.S. nuclear umbrella given to the ROK and thereby avoid the ROK government pursuing its own nuclear weapons.

This project has been a joint effort by the authors, but Chapters 2 through 6 of this report were each initially prepared by one RAND analyst and one Asan analyst.

RAND National Security Research Division

This research was sponsored by the Asan Institute for Policy Studies and conducted within the International Security and Defense Policy Program of the RAND National Security Research Division (NSRD). NSRD conducts research and analysis for the Office of the Secretary of Defense, the U.S. Intelligence Community, the U.S. State Department, allied foreign governments, and foundations.

For more information on the RAND International Security and Defense Policy Program, see www.rand.org/nsrd/isdp or contact the director (contact information is provided on the webpage).

Asan Institute Collaboration

The Asan Institute is an independent, nonpartisan ROK think tank dedicated to undertaking policy-relevant research to foster domestic, regional, and international environments conducive to peace and stability on the Korean Peninsula. RAND and Asan analysts have collaborated on many conferences and other Korean security activities over the years.

Acknowledgments

We appreciate the formal substantive reviews performed by Edward Geist and Yun Kang, of RAND, and Kim Youngjun, of the Korea National Defense University. We also appreciate comments from Kim Young Ho, professor at the Korea National Defense University, Park Changkwon, research fellow emeritus at the Korea Institute for Defense Analyses, and General (ret.) Choi Byung Hyuk, former deputy commander of ROK-U.S. Combined Forces Command.

Summary

In 2021, the RAND Corporation and the Asan Institute produced a report, *Countering the Risks of North Korean Nuclear Weapons* (Bennett et al., 2021). One of the major counters to the risks mentioned in the title has been the U.S. *nuclear umbrella*, which is designed to assure the Republic of Korea (ROK) that the United States will handle North Korean nuclear weapon threats and relieve the ROK of a need for its own nuclear weapons. However, as the North Korean nuclear weapon threat has grown, polls in the ROK (Kim, Kang, and Ham, 2022) show that much of the ROK population is not feeling assured by the U.S. nuclear umbrella and instead favors the ROK developing its own nuclear weapons. In this report, we describe and evaluate options that the ROK and the United States could take to strengthen ROK nuclear assurance.

Issue

North Korea has been vastly expanding its nuclear weapon threat over the past ten years or so and apparently plans to accelerate this process in the future. North Korea has also adopted an extremely hostile campaign of threatening the ROK and the United States with nuclear attacks. China is also vastly expanding its nuclear weapon capabilities and is no longer trusted by most people in the ROK ("Koreans Distrust Chinese More Than Russians, Japanese," 2022).

To counter these threats, the United States provides extended deterrence for the ROK and promises a nuclear umbrella to cover the ROK so that the ROK does not need its own nuclear weapons, the development of which could imperil the Nuclear Non-Proliferation Treaty. This treaty is the foundation of U.S. nuclear nonproliferation policy. The United States has based this nuclear umbrella on a high degree of strategic ambiguity in the belief that this ambiguity will achieve the most-effective deterrence of North Korean aggression.

For nearly seven decades, the U.S. nuclear umbrella was very assuring to the ROK. Now that North Korea poses a serious nuclear weapon threat to both the ROK and the United States, however, and as concerns have risen that the United States could abandon the ROK, many in the ROK are doubting the existing U.S. commitment and seeking more-concrete assurance (Yang, 2023). After all, the United States has not even formally defined the nuclear umbrella.

In short, a U.S. status quo approach to the ROK might lead to ROK development of nuclear weapons, which the United States clearly does not want. Avoiding this outcome could require the United States to face stark choices in changing policies to provide the ROK with nuclear assurance while still providing nuclear assurance to other allies and partners and dealing with the high-priority threats to the United States posed by China and Russia. Those trade-offs are beyond the scope of this report.

Thus, in this report, we take a descriptive approach to identifying the options that are available to both the ROK and the United States to adjust their policies and measures to enhance the strategic clarity of the U.S. nuclear umbrella. Doing so should reassure the ROK that the North Korean nuclear weapon threat can be managed without the ROK having to field its own nuclear weapons at potentially serious costs to the ROK, the United States, and the nonproliferation regime. The report identifies and provides some evaluation of strategy and policy options, force employment options, and nuclear force posture options for both today and in the coming decades. The potential implementation of some of these options has been included in the April 2023 Washington Declaration of U.S. President Joe Biden and ROK President Yoon Suk Yeol.

Approach

This report is a combined effort of the RAND Corporation and the Asan Institute. We start by looking at the nature of the North Korean and Chinese nuclear weapon threats and how North Korea and China might employ those threats. We do so using open literature that describes the quantities and qualities of the nuclear weapons, North Korean and Chinese statements, and previous RAND and Asan research.

We then develop the options for strengthening ROK assurance using our expertise that draws on statements of ROK and U.S. national security experts; knowledge of planned modernization efforts; and knowledge of nuclear forces, nuclear strategy, and nuclear force employment. We describe the feasibility and desirability of these options using open-source information.

We do not seek to be prescriptive but instead to describe options and their relative advantages and disadvantages. Only when an option has substantially greater disadvantages than advantages is that option dismissed.

Key Findings

Our examination of the North Korean and Chinese nuclear weapon threats to the ROK and United States lead us to conclude the following:

- North Korea has already established a nuclear weapon force that could pose an existential threat to the ROK and is on the verge of posing a serious threat to the United States. The North hopes to use its nuclear weapon threat to the United States to help break the ROK-U.S. alliance.[1] The North also hopes to dominate the ROK without having to invade it.[2]
- China also poses very serious nuclear weapon threats to the ROK and the United States and will likely use its nuclear weapons as one means for influencing both countries.
- ROK assurance in the U.S. nuclear umbrella has faltered because of these growing threats and ambiguity in the U.S. commitment to ROK

---

[1] As described in the report, North Korea apparently hopes to undermine the U.S. nuclear umbrella by threatening nuclear attacks on the United States if the United States uses its nuclear weapons to retaliate against North Korean nuclear weapon attacks on the ROK.

[2] A 2023 ROK poll indicates that, when nuclear weapons are included, a significant plurality find North Korea to be militarily superior to the ROK (Lee et al., 2023, pp. 56–58). A 2023 U.S. National Intelligence Estimate argues that the North is highly likely to use this superiority for coercion to "yield political, economic, or military benefits" (National Intelligence Council, 2023). Thus, this dominance would take the form of the ability to coerce the ROK into actions wanted by North Korea rather than North Korean occupation and strong control of the ROK.

security, leading to increased calls for the ROK to develop its own nuclear weapons.

- Because of these developments, the level of strategic ambiguity of the U.S. nuclear umbrella is no longer appropriate for either deterrence or ROK assurance.
- President Biden responded to ROK concerns, in part those voiced by ROK President Yoon, by announcing the Washington Declaration with President Yoon in April 2023; the declaration promises greater strategic clarity. However, the Washington Declaration lacks the implementation details that are needed to truly increase ROK nuclear assurance. The declaration especially lacks details related to the creation of the Nuclear Consultative Group, which would be key to nuclear assurance.
- The United States could pursue strategic clarity akin to the efforts taken by the United States in NATO in the 1960s (McNamara, 1962).
- The United States could commit nuclear weapons to establish some level of parity against the growing, likely existential, North Korean nuclear weapon threat to the ROK. Doing so might avoid a future ROK government decision to produce its own nuclear weapon force.
- ROK nuclear weapon production could lead to international sanctions on the ROK that would seriously damage the ROK economy, cause tremendous political controversy and instability in the ROK and Northeast Asia, and increase global nuclear weapon proliferation, which would be problematic for both the ROK and the United States.

Options to Strengthen ROK Nuclear Assurance

The main function of this report is to present options to be considered for strengthening ROK nuclear assurance. The ROK and United States could implement the following options, which we list from those that would be the easiest to implement to those that would likely be more difficult to implement but have the greatest impact:

1. Implement a dynamic and capable NCG, which could be assisted by a team of strategic advisors, to bring strategic clarity to the U.S. nuclear umbrella extended to the ROK.[3]

2. Educate ROK and U.S. national security personnel on the implications of the North Korean nuclear weapon threat and what can be done about it.

3. Develop more ROK public awareness of the North Korean nuclear weapon threat and the actions that are being taken to counter it. This option could also better explain the serious risks and potential downsides of ROK nuclear weapon development.

4. Shift the focus of conflict planning in the Combined Forces Command to dynamic planning with conventional-nuclear force integration. The Combined Forces Command could use regular tabletop exercises to assist in strategy formulation, which would enhance both defensive and offensive efforts against North Korean nuclear weapon use and thereby strengthen deterrence of that use and ROK nuclear assurance.

5. Establish ROK and U.S. nuclear weapon employment guidelines, exploit the regular tabletop exercises, and seek ROK and U.S. National Command Authority approval of the guidelines.

6. Use a full variety of information, economic, and military coercive measures to induce a North Korean nuclear weapon and critical nuclear material production freeze.

7. Commit some U.S. nuclear weapons to support ROK security. The ROK and United States could use an approach with a four-step, sequential process to establish a degree of parity with the North Korean nuclear weapon threat and seek a North Korean nuclear weapon production freeze.[4] This family of options is designed to

---

[3] President Yoon has been very clear that he thinks strategic clarity is needed to strengthen ROK nuclear assurance. In early 2023, he argued that the "nuclear weapons belong to the U.S., but the planning, information sharing, exercises and training should be carried out jointly by South Korea and the U.S." (Lee H., 2023a).

[4] This four-step process uses some of the principles the United States used to prevent North Atlantic Treaty Organization nuclear proliferation beyond the United Kingdom and France and adds some new ideas.

provide nuclear reassurance while minimizing ROK and regional political turmoil that might otherwise accompany U.S. nuclear weapon deployments in the ROK.[5] The process involves the following four steps:

a. Modernize or build new U.S. tactical nuclear weapon storage in the ROK.

b. Dedicate all or part of the nuclear weapons on a U.S. ballistic missile submarine operating in the Pacific to targeting North Korea.

c. Modernize approximately 100 U.S. tactical nuclear weapons—which the United States otherwise plans to dismantle—at ROK expense. These weapons could then be stored in the United States but would be committed to supporting the ROK and rapidly deployable to the ROK.

d. Deploy a limited number of U.S. tactical nuclear weapons to the ROK to be stored in the prepared nuclear weapon storage facilities.

Option 7, which we characterize as being the most difficult to implement but likely having the greatest impact on ROK nuclear assurance, could be implemented slightly differently from what is proposed here depending on specific ROK and U.S. government requirements. But, if implemented roughly as described, this option could commit up to about 180 U.S. nuclear weapons to ROK security in the next few years; perhaps eight to 12 B61 nuclear bombs could be deployed in the ROK for both symbolic and operational purposes. If ROK and U.S. threats to implement these steps fail to lead to a North Korean nuclear weapon production freeze—failure that we unfortunately expect—further commitments of U.S. nuclear forces in future years could sustain the appearance of nuclear weapon parity with North Korea and avoid the appearance that the ROK needs to produce its own nuclear weapons.

---

[5] For example, rather than the United States immediately deploying tactical nuclear weapons in the ROK, this stepwise approach is designed to demonstrate, especially to the Chinese and to ROK progressives, the rationales for countering the North Korean nuclear weapon buildup and the patience and moderation being shown by the ROK and United States.

Contents

Figure and Tables

Figure

Tables

CHAPTER 1

Introduction

Over at least the past ten years, the Republic of Korea (ROK) has become increasingly uneasy about the significant growth in the North Korean and Chinese nuclear weapon threats.[1] North Korea has also been very active in threatening nuclear weapon use (see, for example, Kim and Smith, 2022) and in provoking the ROK by testing nuclear weapons and the missiles that could be used to deliver those weapons (Jewell, 2022). The United States has sought to assure the ROK against these threats by maintaining a firm alliance with the ROK; this alliance includes an extended deterrence commitment to the ROK and, specifically, a nuclear umbrella to deter adversary use of nuclear weapons against the ROK. But ROK *nuclear assurance*—ROK confidence that the United States will effectively support ROK security— has been declining and has led to increasing interest from the ROK in possessing its own nuclear weapons (Choi and Kim, 2023). The United States is anxious to avoid such a development, fearing that it could undermine the Nuclear Non-Proliferation Treaty, which has been the hallmark of U.S. efforts to prevent global nuclear proliferation.[2]

In this report, we describe options that are available to the United States and the ROK for strengthening ROK nuclear assurance. In this chapter, we begin by describing U.S. extended deterrence and the U.S. nuclear umbrella. We then characterize the differences between nuclear deterrence and nuclear assurance and explain why many in the ROK are concerned about North Korean nuclear weapons despite the likelihood that the North will not launch them. We then describe the issues that affect ROK concerns

---

[1] This chapter was prepared by Bruce W. Bennett and Choi Kang.

[2] Treaty on the Non-Proliferation of Nuclear Weapons, January 7, 1968.

about nuclear assurance. The majority of the report then offers descriptive (not proscriptive) options for strengthening ROK nuclear assurance, including potential changes in ROK and U.S. nuclear policy, strategy, planning, and force posture. These changes would pose stark trade-offs for the United States with its other allies and partners and in fully handling the Russian and Chinese threats; these trade-offs are beyond the scope of this report. We conclude by looking forward to the future; North Korean nuclear forces are likely to become ever more threatening and could require different ROK and U.S. actions from those presented in this report to counter the threats and sustain ROK nuclear assurance.

The U.S. Nuclear Umbrella for the ROK

The United States employs deterrence "to decisively influence the adversary's decision-making calculus in order to prevent hostile actions against U.S. vital interests" (U.S. Department of Defense [DoD], 2006, p. 5). *Direct deterrence* refers to the United States' efforts to defend itself. The U.S. Air Force's Curtis E. Lemay Center (2020) has described *extended deterrence* as

> a commitment to deter and, if necessary, to respond across the spectrum of potential nuclear and non-nuclear scenarios in defense of allies and partners. This commitment is often described as providing a "nuclear umbrella." Extended deterrence also serves as a nonproliferation tool by obviating the need for allies and partners to develop or acquire and field their own nuclear arsenals.

Effectively, the United States is communicating to its allies: "Trust us. If you are threatened by nuclear weapons, we will deal with that threat."

The United States has made many efforts to build that trust with the ROK. The United States entered into a mutual defense treaty with the ROK in 1953 (Mutual Defense Treaty Between the United States and the Republic of Korea, 1953). In support of that treaty, the United States has continuously maintained a significant number of U.S. military personnel based in the ROK and prepared those personnel to defend the ROK and support the flow of reinforcements from the United States in response to any major North Korean attack. In 2022, there were about 30,000 U.S. military personnel deployed in the ROK, more than in any other foreign country except for Germany and Japan (Defense Manpower Data Center, 2022). Additionally, there are more than 100,000 U.S. citizens living in the ROK.[3] The United States has regularly confirmed its offer of a nuclear umbrella to the ROK through, for example, the 2009 U.S.-ROK joint vision for the alliance and the 2022 security consultative meeting between the U.S. Secretary of Defense and the ROK Minister of Defense.[4] Indeed, the U.S. ambassador to Seoul, Philip Goldberg, claimed that the U.S. commitment to extended deterrence was firm and that the U.S. commitment should not be doubted, implying that Seoul's indigenous nuclear development or the redeployment of U.S. tactical nuclear weapons is not a sensible option.[5]

There should be no question that, since 1953, the ROK and the United States have effectively deterred North Korea from invading the ROK a second time or employing its nuclear weapons. The ROK and the United States have tailored their deterrence to prevent these threats. For example, in both the 2018 and the 2022 U.S. Nuclear Posture Reviews, the United States has said, "any nuclear attack by North Korea against the United States or its Allies and partners is unacceptable and will result in the end of that regime" (DoD, 2018; DoD, 2022b). Because North Korean leader Kim Jong-un appears to value nothing as highly as the survival of his regime, this is a powerful deterrence statement.

Still, the United States is concerned that almost all polls on ROK development of nuclear weapons in recent years show that a significant majority of ROK citizens support development of an independent nuclear weapon force. For example, a series of public opinion polls done in the ROK across mul-

---

[3]   These three bases for trust are described in Work (2022). The number of U.S. citizens living in the ROK is from Korean Immigration Service (2022, p. 472).

[4]   The White House's statement on the joint vision says, "We will maintain a robust defense posture, backed by allied capabilities which support both nations' security interests. The continuing commitment of extended deterrence, including the U.S. nuclear umbrella, reinforces this assurance" (White House, 2009). The security consultative meeting "served as an opportunity for the U.S. to reaffirm its strong will to provide extended deterrence to South Korea by using all categories of military capabilities, including nuclear weapons, in the future" (Lee J., 2022).

[5]   Ambassador Goldberg said, "We have this iron-clad commitment. Nobody should have any doubt about that" (Kim H., 2022).

tiple years show this pattern; the percentages of those favoring a ROK independent nuclear weapon force have increased in recent years (Kim, Kang, and Ham, 2022). Another poll that has been conducted for years shows a strong ROK preference for an independent nuclear weapon force but notes that this percentage of popular preference declined from 2021 to 2022 and then again in 2023 (Lee et al., 2023). Regardless of the pattern in the polls, in recent years there appear to have been increasing numbers of ROK policymakers interested in ROK development of nuclear weapons (Lankov, 2023).

ROK trust in the U.S. commitment to ROK security is also an issue of concern. Another recent ROK poll showed that 58 percent of respondents are no longer sure that they can trust U.S. military support against North Korea if it attacks the ROK—the essence of extended deterrence—even in a conventional conflict.[6] However, another poll found that 51 percent of respondents think the United States would exercise nuclear deterrence even if North Korea could target the United States with nuclear weapons (CHEY Institute of Advanced Studies, 2023). And another ROK poll showed that 52 percent of respondents think that the ROK "does not need to build its own nuclear weapons because the U.S. nuclear umbrella policy protects South Korea" (Lee et al., 2023, p. 43). Whatever the actual percentages, a significant fraction of those in the ROK are unsure whether they can trust U.S. extended deterrence. However, many are confident in this deterrence, which provides a viable basis for working on actions to strengthen ROK assurance.

Recognizing these challenges, President Joe Biden and President Yoon Suk Yeol agreed to the Washington Declaration in April 2023 ("Full Text of Washington Declaration Adopted at Yoon-Biden Summit," 2023). The declaration has the potential to strengthen ROK nuclear assurance. A poll (Lee et al., 2023) conducted close to the announcement of the Washington Declaration suggests that it and other developments might help reduce ROK interest in an independent nuclear weapon force.

---

[6] In this poll, 54 percent of respondents said that the United States would intervene only if doing so was in the U.S. interest, whereas 4 percent said that the United States would not intervene. Only 37 percent said that the United States would unconditionally support the ROK (Yang, 2023).

Contrasting Nuclear Deterrence and Nuclear Assurance

Some ROK leaders have been increasingly skeptical of the adequacy of the U.S. nuclear umbrella. In early 2023, President Yoon said, "The so-called 'extended deterrence' also means that the U.S. will take care of everything, so South Korea should not worry, but it is difficult to convince the Korean people to that extent now" (Choi and Kim, 2023). The challenge is that there are important differences between nuclear deterrence and nuclear assurance:

> Nuclear weapons in particular illustrate the complexity of defining the requirements of assurance. Denis Healey, Britain's Defence Minister in the late 1960s, formulated what he called "The Healey Theorem" in order to underscore the difficulty of the assurance aspect of extended deterrence—that is, "it takes only five per cent credibility of American retaliation to deter the Russians, but ninety-five per cent credibility to reassure the Europeans." (Yost, 2009, p. 756)

Why are the ROK leaders and population not fully assured despite North Korea being deterred from nuclear weapon attacks on the ROK? There appear to be the following six principal reasons that will be further addressed in Chapter 2:

- The U.S. nuclear umbrella has required ROK blind trust in a U.S. commitment that lacks a clear definition of its content or scope. This commitment might be sufficient to deter a risk-averse aggressor, but visibility and transparency are often required to reassure potential victims (the ROK people) who are risk averse.
- Kim Jong-un apparently hopes that his developing intercontinental ballistic missile (ICBM) threat will deter U.S. implementation of the nuclear umbrella by threatening U.S. cities in response.
- The United States does not appear to be taking action to prevent North Korea from enhancing the qualitative and quantitative aspects of its nuclear weapon threat, including its delivery means.
- The U.S. withdrawal from Afghanistan was a major shock in the ROK, especially coming in the aftermath of former President Donald Trump's

threats to abandon the ROK-U.S. alliance. The U.S. withdrawal from Vietnam in 1970s is also viewed as a worrisome precedent.

- North Korean military threats against the ROK and United States are becoming increasingly aggressive. Kim Jong-un appears to be feeling increasingly able to exploit the North's "nuclear shadow."[7]
- Russia and China refuse to allow the United Nations (UN) Security Council to act against the North Korean missile tests or nuclear weapon production.

The result is that a growing number of ROK citizens, and especially President Yoon, have been interested in seeing the U.S. nuclear umbrella strengthened to be more visible and give the ROK greater nuclear assurance; the Washington Declaration is a key effort to that end.

Some Issues for Assurance and Deterrence

In planning both assurance of the ROK and deterrence of North Korea, there are several thorny issues for which U.S. policy does not appear to be prepared.

First, who constitutes the "regime" that the Nuclear Posture Reviews threaten will not survive North Korean nuclear weapon use? Would the United States seek to eliminate only Kim Jong-un, potentially allowing his sister, Kim Yo-jong, or one of his children to assume regime leadership? Would the United States seek to eliminate the entire Kim family, potentially allowing another existing North Korean leader or group to assume control of the North and potentially continue any ongoing conflict?[8] Would the United States target Pyongyang to eliminate, perhaps, 90 percent of the

---

[7] An aggressor, such as Kim Jong-un, might carry out coercion or limited attacks hoping that the United States and its allies would be deterred from any major response out of fear of starting an escalatory spiral to nuclear war. See Brewster (2022).

[8] In his discussions with several very senior, elite North Korean escapees, Bruce Bennett was told in 2016 that the regime senior leadership planned for a specific group of about five individuals from outside the Kim family to assume collective leadership in such a case (North Korean escapees, discussions with Bruce Bennett, 2016).

North Korean elites,[9] leaders, and bureaucrats, without whom Kim likely could not rule North Korea even if he personally survived?

A related question is whether the United States would really respond to a limited North Korean use of nuclear weapons by eliminating the regime. Would the United States eliminate the regime if it detonates a single nuclear weapon to cause electromagnetic pulse (EMP) damage to the ROK, an attack that might cause minimal loss of ROK life?[10] Would a North Korean attack on a single ROK military airfield, a type of attack that Kim has threatened, lead to regime elimination efforts by the United States (Kim and Smith, 2022)? If there is any question in these cases, does the United States not require a broader deterrence strategy to prevent such attacks and to provide ROK assurance?

Perhaps the most difficult issue for the ROK and United States is whether to seek to freeze or at least slow the North Korean nuclear weapon buildup rather than deal with the serious consequences of that buildup that might arise in as few as five to ten years. Are the ROK and United States better served by applying a coercive campaign now against the North Korean buildup, risking North Korea retaliation, or by waiting until Kim has built a much larger nuclear weapon force? The fact that North Korea is a severely revisionist country that likely seeks coercive and offensive power against the ROK, and even against the United States, suggests that acting sooner would be better (National Intelligence Council, 2023). Kim's vision seems clear: His cadres received training that

> [t]he dear supreme commander will dominate the world with the nuclear weapons, will make the U.S. apologize and compensate us for decades of bullying our people, and will declare to the entire world that the world's powerful order will be reshaped by the Juche-Korea, not the United States. (Baik, 2019)

Such beliefs are dangerous if Kim also has the nuclear weapons to support them.

---

[9] North Korean escapees provided this estimate (North Korean escapees, discussions with Bruce Bennett, 2016).

[10] For a description of EMP effects, see Bennett et al. (2022, pp. 45–54).

Methodology

This report is a combined effort of the RAND Corporation and the Asan Institute. Chapters 2 through 6 were each initially drafted by a combination of RAND and Asan experts. This approach allowed us to include key open information from both U.S. and ROK sources. Bruce Bennett of RAND and Kang Choi of Asan took the overall lead; Bennett and Choi coordinated the effort, integrated the chapters, and prepared this chapter and the front matter.

This report draws from and summarizes our expertise in nuclear weapon–related threats, policies, and public reactions. We have observed and studied ROK reactions to the growing North Korean and Chinese nuclear weapon threats, and Asan has done a series of public opinion polls on Korean attitudes toward these threats (Kim, Kang, and Ham, 2022). Both RAND and Asan researchers have proposed specific responses to these threats (see, for example, Bennett, 2022a). This report aggregates such previous work with our new thinking on the options available for strengthening ROK nuclear assurance. It is not the purpose of RAND and Asan to propose a specific approach to strengthening ROK nuclear assurance but to identify a variety of options that the U.S. and ROK governments could consider for this purpose. Any eventual U.S. and ROK efforts to strengthen ROK nuclear assurance could involve various options to achieve the desired effect.

This report uses only open information (including information from North Korean escapees) on the North Korean and Chinese nuclear threats and ROK reactions to them. The ROK and U.S. governments may have better information in these areas. We make every effort to characterize the uncertainty in the North Korean and Chinese nuclear weapon-related threats and potential ROK public reaction to them. A renowned former RAND scholar, Roberta Wohlstetter, wrote, "We have to accept the fact of uncertainty and learn to live with it. No magic, in code or otherwise, will provide certainty. Our plans must work without it" (as quoted in Bernstein, 2010).

Organization of This Report

Although several studies have examined these issues (see, for example, Ahn, 2022; Brewer and Dalton, 2023; Go, 2022; and Roberts, 2020), this report provides a new perspective and many new ideas in the following five chapters. In Chapter 2, we characterize the growth in the North Korean nuclear weapon threat, which we believe will be more serious than most recognize and is why we believe that ROK society needs greater nuclear assurance. In Chapters 3 through 5, we consider options for strengthening current ROK nuclear assurance and assess how necessary and effective each option could be. Chapter 3 covers strategic and policy options, including increasing the strategic clarity of the U.S. nuclear umbrella and establishing a coercive campaign to rein in North Korean nuclear weapon production. Chapter 4 addresses force employment planning and execution assurance options, explaining in part how the difficulties in identifying North Korean targets for U.S. nuclear weapons create a demand for a dynamic nuclear employment process more appropriate for ROK-U.S. cooperation. In Chapter 5, we develop nuclear weapon posture and commitment assurance options, including a four-step process for committing U.S. nuclear weapons that is designed to strengthen ROK nuclear assurance and reduce ROK political concerns while providing coercive pressure on North Korea. In Chapter 6, we turn to the changing conditions that we expect will affect ROK nuclear assurance and how nuclear weapon parity could balance the growth in the North Korean nuclear weapon threat with U.S. nuclear weapon commitments to ROK security. In the appendix, we describe our nuclear damage assessment in more detail.

CHAPTER 2

Why the ROK Needs Greater Nuclear Assurance

As described in Chapter 1, many people in the ROK perceive that the existing U.S. nuclear umbrella is insufficient.[1] They find it difficult to trust a vague U.S. nuclear umbrella when the North poses a substantial and potentially existential nuclear weapon threat to the ROK. Although U.S. conventional extended deterrence of the ROK is clear and well demonstrated, the U.S. nuclear umbrella is shrouded in strategic ambiguity. The relatively blind trust that the United States has asked the ROK to have toward the U.S. nuclear umbrella worked for many years, but it is now failing in part because North Korean nuclear weapon capabilities have grown so large and threatening. The United States has failed to deter the North Korean nuclear weapon and delivery system growth and related provocations. Moreover, ROK trust in the United States is undermined by U.S. failure to contain the North Korean ICBM threat to the United States and to fully protect its own military forces deployed in the ROK from potential nuclear weapon attacks.

In this chapter, to provide a basis for considering options for strengthening the ROK nuclear assurance in Chapters 3 through 6, we describe the growing dangers posed by North Korean nuclear weapons and how North Korean nuclear weapons could target the United States, undermining the U.S. nuclear umbrella. These dangers have led the ROK to need greater nuclear assurance. We also examine Chinese nuclear weapon threats and how they are growing. We then identify the reasons why the ROK people

---

[1] This chapter was prepared by Bruce W. Bennett, Cortez Cooper, and Choi Kang, with assistance from Cha Du-hyeogn.

might not trust the U.S. nuclear umbrella. Analogy is made to a similar challenge that the United States faced with its European partners around 1960.

The North Korean Threat

For decades after World War II, North Korea posed primarily a conventional military threat to the ROK, with a particular focus on the potential for a second North Korean invasion of the ROK. But, over the past ten years or so, the North has developed a significant nuclear weapon force. That buildup, coupled with North Korean missile testing, has undercut ROK nuclear assurance. Indeed, President Yoon "said the strategy of 'nuclear umbrella' or 'extended deterrence' is no longer reassuring for the public now that North Korea has developed nuclear weapons and a range of missiles to deliver them" (Cha, 2023).

North Korean Nuclear Weapon Development History

North Korean interest in nuclear weapons started at the end of World War II. Japan brought workers from the Korea Peninsula into many parts of Japan, a significant number of whom were in Hiroshima and Nagasaki when more than 20,000 Koreans apparently died from the U.S. nuclear attacks on those cities. Many Korean survivors were able to testify to the nuclear attack events (Taylor, 2016):

> As the news about the events at Hiroshima and Nagasaki spread throughout the world, nuclear weapons came to be viewed as the ultimate 'doomsday' weapon, a perception that was reinforced by Koreans who had been in Hiroshima and Nagasaki at the time of the bombing. (Bermudez, 2000, p. 184)

Some of the Koreans who returned to North Korea after World War II brought their stories with them. The North Korean leaders apparently recognized the deterrence and coercive leverage that nuclear weapons would offer.

During the Korean War, U.S. threats of nuclear weapon use sharpened North Korean interest in the coercive power of nuclear weapons. These threats against North Korea and China helped achieve the Korean War armistice in 1953.[2] Since the armistice,

> a nuclear inferiority complex has pervaded DPRK [Democratic People's Republic of Korea] strategic thinking and foreign policy, leading DPRK leaders to spend their lives and their nation's resources to make sure that they never again experience this type of coercion.(Bermudez, 2000, p. 185)[3]

The United States introduced nuclear weapons in the ROK in 1958; the number of U.S. nuclear weapons in the ROK grew to over 1,000 by the late 1960s (Kristensen, 2005b). By 1990, those numbers had declined to around 200; all of them were withdrawn as the result of the 1991 order by U.S. President George H. W. Bush to return almost all tactical nuclear weapons from such places as Korea to the United States (Oberdorfer, 1991).

North Korean nuclear development has proceeded since the 1950s. Initially, North Korea pressured the Soviet Union to provide it with information and training (Szalontai and Radchenko, 2006, p. 3). It obtained Soviet help to build a research reactor in the 1960s. Then the North, lacking needed assistance from the Soviet Union or China, built its own small nuclear reactor in the 1980s (Nuclear Threat Initiative, 2018). Although North Korea has had severe electrical energy shortages, as of 2005, "The reactors at Yongbyon—the site that initially attracted world concern about Pyongyang's nuclear intentions—were never hooked up to the country's electrical energy grid, nor are they today. They have been exclusively used for harvesting weapons-grade plutonium" (Eberstadt, 2005). In the 1990s, North Korea obtained the procedures and equipment necessary for producing highly enriched uranium (Hersh, 2003). Pakistani scientist A. Q. Khan said that North Korea was using 3,000 or more centrifuges for uranium enrichment as early as 2002, noting that "Pakistan helped the country with vital machinery, drawings and technical advice for at least six years"

---

[2] The degree to which threats of nuclear weapon use influenced the eventual armistice is debated. Moreover, nuclear threats made throughout the war, and not just once Dwight Eisenhower became the U.S. President, influenced the eventual armistice. See, for example, Dingman (1988–1989) and Foot (1988–1989).

[3] The Democratic People's Republic of Korea is the formal name of North Korea.

(Smith and Warrick, 2009). The efforts gave the North the plutonium and highly enriched uranium fuels needed to make nuclear weapons. According to Khan, he visited North Korea in 1999 and was shown three completed nuclear warheads (Smith and Warrick, 2009); if true, North Korea's nuclear weapon inventory is likely larger than U.S. experts estimated at that time and more than today's estimates, which assume that North Korean nuclear weapon production did not start until 2005 or so. North Korea went on to carry out six nuclear weapon tests from 2006 to 2017 and aggressively build nuclear weapons ("North Korea's Nuclear Programme Going 'Full Steam Ahead,' IAEA Chief Says," 2021).

North Korean Nuclear Weapon Damage Potential

Table 2.1 provides a perspective on the number of casualties that even a single North Korean nuclear weapon could cause to Seoul, Manhattan, or Beijing, assuming that the weapons used have the yields in kilotons of the weapons that North Korea has tested to date. Casualties would depend

TABLE 2.1
The North Korean Counter-City Nuclear Threat

Test Number	Test Date	Yield (kt)[a]	Fatalities and Serious Injuries[a]		
			Seoul	Manhattan	Beijing
1	October 2006	1.4	64,000	79,000	89,000
2	May 2009	5.0	107,000	133,000	150,000
3	February 2013	13.2	243,000	302,000	340,000
4	January 2016	11.2	210,000	261,000	294,000
5	September 2016	18.8	326,000	405,000	456,000
6	September 2017	230.0	2,000,000	2,489,000	2,800,000

NOTE: See the appendix for how these estimates were made.
[a] Estimates from Voytan et al., 2019.

greatly on the yield of the North Korean weapons used. There are various yield estimates of the North Korean nuclear weapon tests, some of which are lower than shown in Table 2.1. But these estimates are established by physical parameters going beyond just the magnitude of the ground shock of the six tests and should therefore be relatively reliable.

North Korea might use an attack on these cities or others as a deterrence or punishment measure, although other cities would likely have lower population density and, thus, lower casualties. Counter-city attacks, referred to as *assured destruction*, were used by the United States for sizing nuclear weapon force requirements in the 1960s.[4] The damage that North Korea could cause with such attacks would be especially extreme if the North used a weapon with a yield like the North's sixth nuclear weapon test. In a war with the ROK and United States, North Korea would likely hold a strategic reserve of nuclear forces targeting ROK and U.S. cities as a means of forcing war termination if the North begins to lose the conflict.

But in late 2022, North Korea was very clear about its nuclear targeting plans for early in a conflict. It said that the flurry of recent tactical missiles tests "simulated targeting military command facilities, striking main ports, and neutralising airports in the South" (Kim and Smith, 2022). Neutralizing a military airfield with scattered shelters for fighter aircraft cannot be done with a single 20 kt weapon; it would require a nuclear weapon of at least 250 to 500 kt.[5] The same is true of a major seaport. These requirements imply that North Korea is *not* talking about tactical nuclear weapons being

---

[4] Enthoven and Smith (2005, p. 207), who developed U.S. Secretary of Defense Robert McNamara's force requirements in the early 1960s, explain in their book *How Much Is Enough*:

> Basically, U.S. strategic offensive forces were sized according to their ability to destroy the Soviet Union as a viable nation in a retaliatory strike. The level of destruction required—20 to 25 percent of the Soviet population and 50 percent of Soviet industry, commonly called our "assured-destruction" capability—was based on a judgment reached by the Secretary of Defense and accepted by the President, by the Congress, and apparently by the general public as well.

[5] In the late 1970s and the 1980s, RAND conducted many studies of targeting U.S. nuclear weapons against major Soviet targets. One of the conclusions of the analysts doing those studies was that, even with the Poseidon 40 kt nuclear weapon, multiple warheads were required to neutralize most Soviet military airfields (Bruce Bennett, unpublished research, 1976–1980).

small nuclear weapons, as many seem to assume, but rather about weapons that would target the ROK and other theater locations (potentially Japan and China). Making larger yield weapons small enough to fit on a KN-25, as Kim has suggested will require a serious nuclear weapon miniaturization effort that the North is presumably making.

North Korean Nuclear Weapon Inventory

North Korea makes a serious effort to deny the outside world information on its nuclear weapon inventory. Therefore, most open estimates of this inventory are largely based on the amount of critical nuclear material (CNM) that North Korea has produced or is likely producing in its nuclear reactor and uranium enrichment facilities and how much of this material is required to produce a nuclear weapon. Frequently, the amount of CNM produced by North Korea is given in terms of the number of nuclear weapons that could be made from that CNM.

Several leading academic and scientific experts perceive that North Korea has produced limited amounts of CNM cumulatively and will continue to produce modest amounts each year. For example, Sig Hecker, a former Los Alamos National Laboratory director and the outside scientist who has been to the North Korean Yongbyon nuclear complex more than probably any other outsider, wrote that he thought that North Korea had sufficient CNM to produce ten to 28 nuclear weapons (a median of 19) at the time and to produce six more per year (Hecker, Braun, and Lawrence, 2016). In April 2021, Hecker did an interview in which he claimed that North Korea had CNM for 20 to 60 number weapons, with "the most likely number being 45" ("Estimating North Korea's Nuclear Stockpiles," 2021). The growth from a median of 19 at the end of 2016 to 45 in early 2021 would reflect a growth of 26 nuclear weapons of CNM produced in just over four years, or about six nuclear weapons per year. In contrast, some academic and scientific experts think that North Korea had not converted its CNM into any more than ten to 20 actual nuclear weapons as of 2021 (Kristensen and Korda, 2021b, p. 222).

Alternatively, according to the Council on Foreign Relations (2022) and a Korean media source (Jeong, Lee, and Kim, 2017), the U.S. and ROK intelligence communities estimated that North Korea had produced enough

CNM for up to 60 nuclear weapons by 2017 and could produce CNM for 12 more nuclear weapons per year. This "up to 60" estimate clearly reflects a range and could equate to a median estimate of 50 by mid-2017; at 12 more per year, North Korea would have 116 nuclear weapons as of 2023. Meanwhile, previous RAND and Asan work suggests that the maximum amount of CNM could be even higher, starting from the Council on Foreign Relations estimate of enough for 60 nuclear weapons in mid-2017 and increasing at 18 nuclear weapons per year based on extra uranium enrichment capability potentially being available (Bennett et al., 2021, p. 37). Figure 2.1 compares these estimates of CNM availability through 2035.

These estimates assume a constant growth rate into the future and thus could be conservative if the North follows Kim Jong-un's assertions that "he will 'exponentially increase' nuclear weapon production in 2023" (Zwirko, 2023a) and that he will scale "up production of weapon-grade nuclear material to grow the country's arsenal" (Shin, 2023a). Consistent with Kim's asser-

FIGURE 2.1
The Growing North Korean Nuclear Weapon Threat?

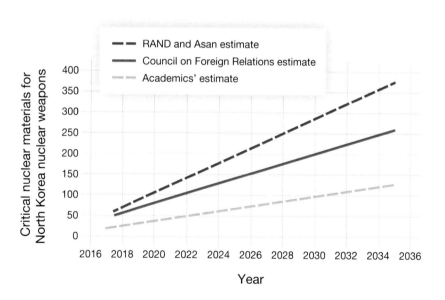

SOURCES: Uses information from "Estimating North Korea's Nuclear Stockpiles," 2021; Bennett et al., 2021, p. 37; Council on Foreign Relations, 2022; Hecker, Braun, and Lawrence, 2016; Jeong, Lee, and Kim, 2017; Kristensen and Korda, 2021b, p. 222.

tions, the North has expanded the size of the uranium enrichment facility at Yongbyon, which might involve added highly enriched uranium production capacity. As a result, even these estimates could be low. The chief of the International Atomic Energy Agency has said that the North's "nuclear programme goes full steam ahead with work on plutonium separation, uranium enrichment and other activities" ("North Korea's Nuclear Programme Going 'Full Steam Ahead,' IAEA Chief Says," 2021). Each of these estimates is uncertain, with a margin of error of at least 20 to 30 percent.

Some may argue that these estimates are high because the North will not keep building CNM or nuclear weapons from the CNM. However, in speaking about the KN-25 missiles, Kim Jong-un said that "30 units will be assigned tactical nuclear warheads eventually and are capable of striking anywhere in South Korea" (Panda, 2023). Each KN-25 launcher shown with that report was designed to carry six KN-25 missiles, which would amount to 180 North Korean nuclear weapons oriented on targets primarily in the ROK because the maximum range of the KN-25 is only about 350 km (not enough to reach Japan) (Panda, 2023). But the KN-25 is not the North's best short-range missile: The KN-23, its Iskander-like missile, is more capable. If Kim plans to build 180 KN-25s with nuclear weapons, it must be expected that he also plans to build at least 100 to 150 KN-23 missiles with nuclear weapons. North Korea would undoubtedly also build nuclear weapons for missiles that can reach the United States, Japan, and likely China (Myers, 2022). Thus, Kim Jong-un appears to be planning a force of at least 300 to 500 nuclear weapons, which are numbers beyond the current expectations of the security community. As shown in Figure 2.1, the 300-weapon threshold could almost be reached in 2030 using the straight-line RAND and Asan projection with no increase in North Korean nuclear weapon production. If, instead, North Korea doubles its nuclear weapon production from 2025 on, it would achieve 300 nuclear weapons by 2028 using the RAND and Asan projection and by 2032 using the Council on Foreign Relations projection.

These estimates assume North Korean indigenous efforts without any significant outside help or added capabilities. But North Korea introduced a very advanced series of new missiles from 2019 to 2022, moving at a pace that belies the assumption of little outside assistance. Many of these missiles appear to be designed to carry nuclear weapons. Whether these developments reflect outside assistance or simply major advances by the North

Korean scientists, such advances could be mirrored by advances in the North Korean nuclear weapon production that is more rapid than suggested by the estimates shown in Figure 2.1.

North Korean Nuclear Weapon Delivery Means

Traditionally, it has been assumed that North Korea would use ballistic missiles, such as its Scuds, to deliver nuclear weapons. North Korea has fielded far more ballistic missiles than the number of nuclear weapons it possesses, apparently planning to also use ballistic missiles to deliver conventional munitions (including submunitions) and, likely, chemical weapons. Because ballistic missile testing has proven far less sensitive than nuclear weapon testing, North Korea has actively tested these missiles, including some 95 ballistic and other missiles tested in 2022 (Choe, 2023).

North Korean work on ballistic missiles began in the 1960s. The North did early work with FROG missiles and Scud missiles, the former obtained from the Soviet Union and the latter obtained from Egypt (Nuclear Threat Initiative, 2020). Ballistic missiles appeared to be a rapid way to deliver an attack and had the potential for overcoming or exhausting early missile defenses. The Scud missiles can reach targets in the ROK and allow for a payload and warhead size that could accommodate nuclear weapons if the North masters a fair degree of nuclear weapon miniaturization. The North then evolved into longer-range missiles—such as the NoDong, which could reach Japan—and tried to build the Musudan missile for reaching such targets as Guam. Most tests of the Musudan missile failed. North Korea may have 500 to 600 Scuds, and perhaps 300 NoDongs (Missile Defense Project, 2021a).

As ROK and U.S. missile defenses improved, so did North Korean ballistic missiles. These missile defense improvements did not provide the level of nuclear assurance that the United States had hoped for.[6] For attacks in Northeast Asia, the North decided to build quasi-ballistic missiles—the KN-23, KN-24, and KN-25—that only partially fly a ballistic trajectory and maneuver en route to a target. This maneuverability makes it more difficult

---

[6] At one time, the United States had hoped that missile defenses would convince adversaries to abandon ballistic missile delivery of nuclear weapons. See DoD (2002, p. 3).

for even advanced ROK and U.S. missile defenses to intercept them (Delory, Bondaz, and Maire, 2023). As of 2023, there do not appear to be reliable estimates of how many of these new missiles North Korea has already produced or acquired. Still, as noted previously, Kim Jong-un has indicated that North Korea will produce at least 180 KN-25 missiles for nuclear weapon delivery on the peninsula; it would not be surprising to see North Korea build inventories of several hundred KN-23 and KN-24 missiles. North Korea has also built and tested the Hwasong-12, which can reach Guam, and several ICBMs, which appear capable of delivering nuclear weapons to the United States.

North Korea's interest in nuclear weapon delivery has not been limited to ballistic missiles. In 2022, North Korea has also tested several cruise missiles (Zwirko, 2023a). And North Korea appears to have been actively developing drone aircraft, some of which may be large enough to carry North Korean nuclear weapons. These other delivery means complicate ROK and U.S. efforts to defend against North Korean delivery of nuclear weapons.

North Korean Objectives for Its Nuclear Weapons

The North Korean regime's primary objective is regime survival in control of North Korea. Historically, the regime argued that nuclear weapons had only a defensive purpose, seeking to secure regime survival by deterring foreign intervention and threatening to punish any intervention, should deterrence fail.[7] As shown in Table 2.1, North Korea would not require dozens of nuclear weapons for such a purpose. Neither the ROK nor the United States have much to gain from taking control of North Korea and have much to potentially lose even before even considering the North's nuclear weapon threat, much as Russia has illustrated with its attempts to assert control over Ukraine and as the United States learned with its efforts to assert control over Iraq. Thus, even a limited North Korean nuclear weapon threat—perhaps ten to 20 nuclear weapons—would likely suffice to deter ROK or

---

[7] North Korea "presents its nuclear arsenal as part of a defensive, rather than offensive, strategy: it frames the programme as a response to the risk of a decapitation strike mounted by the United States and its allies, especially South Korea" (Allard, Duchâtel, and Godement, 2017).

U.S. efforts to suddenly invade North Korea. A North Korean attack with 50 to 100-plus nuclear weapons, as the North likely has as of 2023, could be considered an existential threat to the ROK. A nuclear attack does not have to kill everyone in the ROK to have such an effect; the primary damage of casualties and physical damage would reverberate through ROK society, causing secondary damage by breaking societal interdependencies and possibly leading to a breakdown of many aspects of ROK society.

Although North Korea has not abandoned this purported defensive purpose, its expansion of its nuclear arsenal beyond these minimal levels suggests that the North also has an offensive purpose for its nuclear weapon force. North Korean nuclear weapons form the core of an evolving strategic framework that is meant to allow the regime in Pyongyang to dominate the ROK strategically. The North will want this dominance to fight a major war with the ROK if needed and to otherwise give it coercive leverage against the ROK in peacetime. Since the latter part of 2022, North Korea has made it very clear that it is building a large nuclear weapon force to give it a serious offensive nuclear weapon capability against the ROK, with particular focus on destroying major ROK military targets that are essential to supporting the ROK superior conventional military forces: airfields, ports, and military command and control (Kim and Smith, 2022). Doing so could tip the balance of conventional conflict on the peninsula. The North appears to be preparing to use nuclear weapons against Japan in such a contingency, hoping to force Japan to disallow U.S. force deployment to the ROK. To achieve these goals, North Korea's "theory of victory" involves at least some form of decoupling between the ROK and the United States.

Not surprisingly, in September 2022 North Korea announced a new law enshrining a broader nuclear doctrine and strategy. The new doctrine is increasingly offensive and includes several conditions for North Korean nuclear weapon use, "which don't even require an adversary to attack the DPRK"; the doctrine "justifies the pre-emptive use of DPRK nuclear weapons in response to an extremely wide range of circumstances . . . even in cases where an adversary isn't planning to use nuclear weapons against North Korea" (O'Carroll, 2022). The law gives North Korean nuclear forces "a secondary nuclear weapon goal in addition to their primary objective of 'preventing' and 'deterring' war: To 'win' a war if deterrence 'fails'" (Kim J., 2022). Because Kim Jong-un gets to determine when deterrence is failing, these provisions could become very offensive, supporting a North Korean "nuclear shadow" with a threat of limited nuclear attacks that risk escalation to major war (Brewster, 2022).

North Korea's aggressive pursuit of ICBM's might in part be defensive and designed to deter U.S.-initiated attacks on North Korea. But Kim appears particularly intent on challenging the U.S. nuclear umbrella by being able to attack U.S. cities with nuclear weapons if the United States uses nuclear weapons to respond to North Korean nuclear attacks against the ROK. Kim apparently hopes that by decoupling ROK and U.S. interests, he can also decouple the ROK-U.S. alliance. Kim might be hoping that he can get the United States to at least tacitly recognize North Korea as a nuclear weapon state; some in the United States have started to advocate for this recognition (Lewis, 2022). U.S. decisionmakers must be careful with such a position; it would likely stoke fears of abandonment in both the ROK and Japan.

U.S. Failure to Implement Passive Defenses in the ROK

Some ROK personnel are curious about why the United States has not provided more protective measures for its forces in the ROK. Consolidating many of the U.S. military bases in the ROK into Camp Humphreys has placed many of the U.S. forces in the ROK at a single location that a nuclear weapon with the yield of the North's sixth nuclear test could largely destroy. Not surprisingly, North Korea has designated Camp Humphreys as "our military's foremost strike target" (Park, 2017, p. 4). The major U.S. airfields in the ROK—Osan and Kunsan—would also presumably be major North Korean targets. These facilities are protected by U.S. air and missile defenses. But ROK personnel are surprised to find few blast or fallout shelters at the major U.S. bases in Korea. They were also surprised to find no substantial dispersal of selected U.S. military equipment to neighboring ROK military bases or airfields to afford survivability in the case of North Korean nuclear weapon attack, especially a surprise attack. This lack of U.S. protective defenses undermines ROK trust of the United States to handle the North Korean nuclear weapon threat to the ROK because the United States does not appear to be adequately handling the North Korean nuclear weapon threat to even the U.S. military forces in the ROK.

The Chinese Threat

China's strategic interests on the Korean Peninsula encompass economic, diplomatic, and security objectives that can be broadly gathered under two overarching goals: (1) to deter conflict or instability on the peninsula that might spill over China's borders or imperil Chinese economic interests and (2) to shape, or even cause and control, changes to the status quo on the peninsula that might affect the regional balance of power.[8] Although these larger objectives do not necessarily conflict with ROK or U.S.-ROK alliance interests, Chinese actions in response to or in preparation to defend against threats to these interests would likely present significant challenges for the ROK and the alliance in addressing the North Korean nuclear threat.

Additionally, China has developed a wide variety of tools to protect its interests on the peninsula, including conventional and strategic military forces and capabilities. China's chief means of responding to developments that threaten its interests on the peninsula have been economic, via carrots and sticks directed at both Seoul and Pyongyang, but, in the future, Beijing might increasingly turn to its military toolkit to shape or respond to events on the peninsula.[9] Chinese President Xi Jinping's major restructuring of the People's Liberation Army (PLA), which was enacted in late 2015, created the joint Northern Theater Command, specifically designed to address threats to Chinese interests on the Korean Peninsula (Burke and Chan, 2019). Even absent the North Korean threat, China will have an increasing number of arrows in its military quiver to affect ROK and alliance decisionmaking.

China–North Korea Mutual Defense and Its Applications

Historically, the principal mechanism the Chinese Communist Party (CCP) employs to maintain its interests on the Korean Peninsula is the Treaty of

---

[8] For a discussion of broader Chinese strategic objectives and the mechanisms for achieving these, see Scobell (2020).

[9] For background on Chinese economic coercion and punishment directed at the ROK following its deployment of a U.S. Terminal High Altitude Area Defense (THAAD) system in 2016, see Meick and Salidjanova (2017). Beijing also upholds international sanctions against Pyongyang, although its commitment to their enforcement is questionable. See Albert (2019).

Co-operation, Friendship, and Mutual Assistance Between the People's Republic of China and the Democratic People's Republic of Korea, which was signed in 1961 and renewed for another 20 years in 2021. Article 2 of the treaty serves as a mutual defense arrangement between the parties and stands as the only such agreement that either state has with any other state. Interpretations of when and how the treaty would be invoked, however, have varied as the relationship between Beijing and Pyongyang has evolved and as PRC-ROK economic ties have grown. Since roughly 2010, China has indicated, and most regional experts assess, that China would not come to North Korea's aid in a conflict initiated by Pyongyang, but would stand with North Korea should the ROK or the U.S.-ROK alliance initiate hostilities (Denyer and Erickson, 2017; Panda, 2017). In essence, Beijing seeks to simultaneously deter ROK and U.S. actions to undermine the North Korean regime or forcefully unify Korea under ROK control and restrain North Korean aggression against the ROK. Prevailing interpretations of the treaty and of China's general approach to its relationships with the key actors on the peninsula raise several questions when applied to scenarios that might play out in the future. To this point, Beijing has failed to constrain Pyongyang's nuclear ambitions; even if Beijing refrains from siding with North Korea in a case in which Pyongyang initiates military action against the ROK, the response of the alliance to such an attack would call into question Beijing's ability to shape and control outcomes on the peninsula. In turn, such a conflict might bring the PLA into play with both conventional and nuclear forces at Beijing's disposal to protect China's borders and compel parties to the conflict to behave in ways consonant with Beijing's interests. Chinese actions might well involve coercive pressure on Pyongyang to cease hostilities but could also involve threats against the alliance to avoid expanding the conflict toward forceful eradication of the North Korean state. Any conflict, however initiated, that results in a strengthened U.S.-ROK alliance on a peninsula unified under alliance terms would likely be viewed by Beijing as detrimental to its strategic interests.[10]

In a perhaps more likely scenario, Chinese actions because of political instability or regime collapse in North Korea could pose a risk to the

---

[10] For Beijing's evolving views regarding U.S. regional alliance structures, see Scobell et al. (2020).

ROK's and the alliance's efforts to impose order and protect their interests. Although Chinese objectives in such a scenario to secure its own borders and reduce the risk from North Korean nuclear weapons and facilities might align with alliance goals, Beijing's perceptions of ROK or alliance activities could drive China to respond militarily in ways not dissimilar to those described in the conflict scenario above. Either through strategic misunderstanding or because of a perception on Beijing's part that the alliance sought to consolidate control of the peninsula without China's vote in the process, China and the alliance could come to loggerheads.[11] With growing strategic and conventional military clout, Beijing could pose a significant threat to Seoul and complicate U.S. extended deterrence efforts. Because of the trajectory of the PRC-U.S. relationship and Chinese antipathy for strengthening U.S. alliance structures in the region, the probability of a negative outcome in this scenario increases.

Even if crisis or conflict scenarios as described above do not materialize, peacetime trends indicate growing risks of coercive Chinese behavior toward the alliance and continued acceptance of a growing North Korean nuclear arsenal. Although China's stated policy opposes nuclear weapons on the peninsula, Chinese entities continue to aid various aspects of Pyongyang's nuclear weapon program (Kerr, 2023). At the same time, China has proven ready to use the coercive and punitive tools at its disposal to deter actions by the ROK and the alliance to strengthen alliance capabilities on the peninsula. Beijing's response of economic coercion to Seoul's deployment of a U.S. THAAD is the foremost example of economic levers employed to this end. With increasing concern about U.S. willingness and capability to block China's ascendance as the preeminent Indo-Pacific power in a multipolar order, China's military might and growing nuclear arsenal could be employed to similar ends (see, for example, Beauchamp-Mustafaga et al., 2021). Beijing is clearly more concerned about a strengthened U.S.-ROK alliance and inherent advances in alliance military capability on the peninsula than it is about Pyongyang's growing nuclear arsenal (Scobell et al., 2020). Examining Beijing's strategic deterrence concepts and its views of the threats posed by the U.S. facilitates an understanding of this dynamic.

---

[11] For a concise discussion of China's concerns about further consolidation of U.S. power in the region and on the peninsula, see Vu (2021).

Chinese Threat Perceptions and Strategic Deterrence Concept

Since the end of the Cold War, China has viewed U.S. power and influence as the primary obstacle to successful achievement of long-term CCP objectives. Beijing perceives Washington as a capitalist hegemon in decline that is increasingly dangerous in seeking to maintain its position and is focused on containing China's rise through military power and a web of anti-China alliances and partnerships (Savkov, 2020). To shape the geopolitical environment in opposition to this perceived containment and deter the involvement of regional actors in alliance building and other security arrangements with the United States, China pursues a multidimensional path to strategic deterrence that often involves coercive and punitive measures.

The Chinese perspective on strategic deterrence has evolved along with PLA capabilities. Whereas Chinese authors in the 1990s discussed nuclear weapons as the cornerstone of strategic deterrence, *strategic deterrence* today has a broader definition and includes all components of comprehensive national power (Zhou and Yun, 2004). These components include military forces, economic power, diplomatic influence, scientific and technological capabilities, and political and cultural unity, which serve to compel or deter opponents (Peng and Yao, 2005). The major change over the past decade in terms of deterrence approach and escalation dynamics is that Beijing appears increasingly willing to instigate change rather than react to it (Scobell et al., 2020). Although cautious in applying major military force to resolve regional disputes, China has shown increased risk acceptance for actions below the threshold of war. There are several reasons for this risk acceptance, but Beijing most likely is choosing this path because of poor international receptivity of Beijing's soft power and a perception that the United States has instigated a comprehensive strategic rivalry bent on stymying Beijing's grand strategy. Beijing thus views strategic deterrence as not only latent capabilities to dissuade an adversary from certain actions but also the active employment of certain capabilities to coerce or compel opponents to change course and accede to Chinese demands.

PLA analyses on the components of strategic deterrence include conventional and nuclear forces, as well as space and information capabilities (Shou, 2013). The nuclear aspect of strategic deterrence leverages the destructive threat of nuclear weapons to coerce or compel an adversary to

26

reassess a course of action that runs contrary to Beijing's strategic objectives (Xiao, 2020). China continues to officially adhere to a "no first use" nuclear weapon policy but seeks assured retaliation capability for its nuclear force against any adversary as part of its strategic deterrence concept. In keeping with its approach to strategic deterrence, trends in Chinese nuclear force modernization and restructuring indicate that Beijing's approach to assured retaliation vis-à-vis the United States potentially provides weapon numbers and capabilities to compel or coerce regional actors and cause them to question the viability of U.S. extended deterrence.

China's Nuclear Forces

Although China's approach to strategic deterrence involves all aspects of China's party-army-state apparatus, developments in the nuclear force are most salient for considering threats to U.S. extended deterrence and assurance to allies. For roughly half of a century following initial nuclear tests in the 1960s, China fielded only a small number of nuclear weapons—a so-called minimum deterrence force capable, in Beijing's eyes, of deterring the United States or Russia from nuclear blackmail or coercion. A small number of ICBMs were under the control of the PLA Second Artillery, which became the PLA Rocket Force (PLARF) following PLA restructuring in 2015, a service with effectively the same status as the PLA Army, Navy, and Air Force. Shortly after this development, Western analysts following Chinese nuclear force developments openly abandoned the notion of a minimum deterrent force and noted a sharp growth in PLA nuclear systems and capabilities, and not only within the PLARF. The PLA is clearly fielding a triad of land-, sea-, and air-based systems with increased mobility, survivability, and lethal accuracy (Demirjian, 2022).

For decades, the Second Artillery had fielded just over 20 DF-31 ICBMs; since around 2019, the PLARF has fielded the road- and possibly rail-mobile, 15,000-km-range DF-41, which likely mounts multiple independent reentry vehicles to increase the number of warheads delivered by a single missile (Logan, 2019). Added to the existing DF-31 fleet, the increased number of warheads that can target the United States (and that the United States must target in return) dramatically changes the deterrence equation. Recent reporting on China's construction of up to 300 new ICBM silos in western

China indicates that a combination of mobile and silo-based systems, which could deliver a substantially increased number of warheads, will complicate the job of U.S. and allied strategists and planners as they consider deterrent options (Atwood and Hansler, 2021).

Chinese nuclear force expansion includes six Type 094 *Jin*-class ballistic missile submarines equipped with 12 JL-2 or JL-3 submarine-launched ballistic missiles each; a quieter Type 096 ballistic missile submarine that will deploy these missiles is under construction (DoD, 2022b; U.S. Office of the Secretary of Defense, 2021). These missiles are also expected to mount multiple independent reentry vehicles (Missile Defense Project, 2021c). This naval arm of the triad will very likely be able to conduct a constant deterrence patrol. On the air force side of the triad, the PLA has reportedly deployed the H-6N bomber, which can fire an air-launched ballistic missile (U.S. Office of the Secretary of Defense, 2021). The PLA Air Force also has a new strategic bomber in the works as of 2023. The H-20 reportedly will incorporate stealth technology, have a range of 8,500 km, and be capable of carrying both conventional and nuclear payloads (Chan, 2022).

This major expansion of nuclear forces indicates that China's nuclear strategy is evolving. In the parlance of Chinese military strategy, the force has moved to a "moderate nuclear deterrence" with "sufficient and effective" capability to assure a high level of retaliation against nuclear states that might threaten strategic attacks against China (Peng and Yao, 2005). There are no clear CCP statements that indicate why this shift is underway. It is possible that Chinese leaders perceive, or that PLA Air Force leadership has successfully argued, that a larger, diverse force is required to launch an effective counterstrike after an adversary's first strike and in the face of proliferating missile defenses. China also perceives threats from multiple directions; advances in the arsenals of India, Russia, and the United States perhaps create a deterrence problem that Beijing assesses can only be addressed by a force that achieves some level of strategic parity.

It is also possible that Beijing assesses that employment of broader conventional coercive mechanisms (military and otherwise) are only credible if China's nuclear force is on par with its major adversary. This possibility is of particular concern when considering ROK and alliance options to address the North Korean threat when such options could draw Beijing's ire. The *Science of Second Artillery Campaigns*, an internal PLA document that serves as a handbook to guide missile force personnel thinking on missile operations, outlines an escalatory framework that likely remains a guide for strategic deterrence activities that would involve the PLARF (*The Science of Second Artillery Campaigns*, 2003). This ladder framework includes escalating nuclear force activities from elevated alert status, to capability demonstrations, to test launches near adversary territory, to announced lowering of nuclear use thresholds. Triggers for movement up or down the ladder remain ambiguous, but the Chinese have clearly developed options for coercive activities involving the nuclear force as part of larger deterrence campaigns.

Implications for Seoul and Washington

The 2022 DoD report on China's military power succinctly summarized the changing nuclear threat landscape:

> In 2020, the DoD estimated China's operational nuclear warhead stockpile was in the low-200s and expected to at least double by 2030. However, Beijing probably accelerated its nuclear expansion, and DoD estimates this stockpile has now surpassed 400 operational nuclear warheads. By 2030, DoD estimates that the PRC will have about 1,000 operational nuclear warheads, most of which will be fielded on systems capable of ranging the continental United States (CONUS). . . . If China continues the pace of its nuclear expansion, it could field a stockpile of about 1,500 warheads by its 2035 timeline. (U.S. Office of the Secretary of Defense, 2022, pp. 97–98)

This estimate for 2035 would be in line with the numbers of warheads allowed to the United States and Russia under the New START (Strategic Arms Reduction Treaty) agreement (U.S. Department of State, undated).

The reality of such a large, capable force will increasingly complicate ROK and alliance plans and activities to assure ROK leaders and citizenry that U.S. extended deterrence can be effective against the North Korean nuclear menace or against a future threat from a more muscular China. The threat of PRC coercive pressure against the ROK or action against the alliance will almost certainly come into play when decisions are made regarding deployment of weapons systems to the peninsula, whether through additional missile defenses, actual nuclear delivery systems, or a combination of both. In other cases, China might be supportive of developments that strengthen ROK capabilities but undermine the alliance. It remains unknown how Beijing might react to the development of an indigenous ROK nuclear weapon program; if such an outcome irreparably damaged the U.S.-ROK alliance, Beijing might be inclined to tacit acceptance of a more evenly "nuclearized" peninsula that excluded U.S. forces on Beijing's flank.

The Chinese challenge to ROK and alliance freedom of action is not lost on ROK citizens and will likely be reflected both in ROK polity and decisions regarding nuclear assurance activities. Although the ROK has recognized for years that China was seeking regional preeminence, ROK attitudes toward the gravity of this situation have changed in recent years. In August 2022, *JoongAng Ilbo* released the results of a poll of ROK citizens in which it found that "90.2 percent of respondents said they didn't consider China a reliable partner, the highest level of distrust for any country" ("Koreans Distrust Chinese More Than Russians, Japanese," 2022). The ROK attitude toward China is not just an issue of distrust:

> A plurality of South Koreans (46%) cites North Korea as the biggest current threat to South Korea, and 33 percent say the same about China. . . . Yet when asked to assess the threat landscape ten years from now, there is a marked shift. A majority (56%) say China will pose the biggest threat to South Korea, while just 22 percent say it will be North Korea. (Dalton, Friedhoff, and Kim, 2022, p. 12)

Trends in the geostrategic environment will require increased U.S. efforts to reassure the ROK population that the United States can deter nuclear threats to Seoul and manage escalation in the event of conflict.

ROK Interest in Strong Assurance

North Korea has built a nuclear weapon force that probably already poses an existential threat to the ROK. Kim Jong-un's missile and nuclear weapon tests and his fiery rhetoric about using nuclear weapons have convinced more and more ROK citizens that they need very strong assurance that North Korean use of nuclear weapons can be deterred and that, if deterrence fails, North Korean nuclear weapon use can be defeated with minimal damage to the ROK. However, as noted previously in this chapter, North Korean nuclear weapon forces are large enough and qualitatively advanced enough to make difficult any ROK efforts to prevent North Korean nuclear weapon delivery. As it becomes clearer that the ROK and United States are unable to shield the ROK from damage caused by a North Korean nuclear weapon strike (i.e., deterrence by denial appears to be failing), many in the ROK therefore feel that a nuclear weapon retaliation threat (i.e., deterrence by punishment) is needed to deter North Korea. They worry that the United States has been unwilling to promise such a retaliation and that the ROK might not be able to count on the United States to execute such a retaliation when the North is able to threaten a nuclear attack on the United States. These and other concerns have been a factor in a majority of the ROK population wanting an independent ROK nuclear weapon force as a more reliable security guarantee.

As introduced in Chapter 1, there are six major challenges disrupting ROK nuclear assurance: (1) the strategic ambiguity of the U.S. nuclear umbrella, (2) the potential that the United States will abandon its nuclear umbrella once North Korea can directly target the United States, (3) continued North Korean production and testing of nuclear weapons and their delivery means, (4) the potential that the United States could be perceived as abandoning the ROK as an ally as it did Afghanistan, (5) the North Korean nuclear shadow facilitating North Korean provocations and making North Korea even more aggressive over time, and (6) China and Russia preventing the UN Security Council from taking action against continuing North Korean provocations and violations of previous UN Security Council Resolutions. In the next section, we describe these six challenges in more detail.

Strategic Ambiguity of the Nuclear Umbrella

When referring to the nuclear umbrella component of its extended deterrence for the ROK, the United States usually says that it is providing a nuclear umbrella for the ROK without defining what that umbrella is. For example, the 2009 U.S. and the ROK announcement of a "joint vision for the alliance of the United States of America and the Republic of Korea" said, in part,

We will maintain a robust defense posture, backed by allied capabilities which support both nations' security interests. The continuing commitment of extended deterrence, including the U.S. nuclear
umbrella, reinforces this assurance. (White House, 2009)

The role of U.S. nuclear weapons in the U.S. nuclear umbrella is in part
obscured by the U.S. deterrence statement against North Korean nuclear
weapon use referenced in Chapter 1: "Any nuclear attack by North Korea
against the United States or its Allies and partners is unacceptable and will
result in the end of that regime" (DoD, 2022b). This statement is viewed
by many in the ROK as inadequate because the United States does not
commit to using nuclear weapons in response to North Korean use of
nuclear weapons.

The current U.S. nuclear umbrella policy can accurately be characterized
as calculated ambiguity. In other words, in theory, North Korea knows that
the United States intends to use nuclear weapons against the North under
certain circumstances, but the North does not know how or when. There
are those who argue that this makes the deterrence factor more effective. To
quote Matthew Costlow of the National Institute for Public Policy,

U.S. nuclear declaratory policy requires an adversary to gamble twice.
First, they gamble that the United States will not respond to an attack
with its nuclear forces, and second, that the attack will achieve its goals
in the face of a U.S. conventional response. These gambles, enabled by
a policy of calculated ambiguity, can aid deterrence by increasing an
adversary's uncertainty regarding the type and consequences of a U.S.
response. (Costlow, 2021)

Thus, even though the U.S. President may in practice be reluctant to execute
a nuclear weapon response against some North Korean aggressions, and
especially limited nuclear attacks, Kim cannot be sure—corresponding to
the Healey Theorem presented in Chapter 1 (Yost, 2009). There are those
who argue that this will make the leadership in North Korea more hesitant
to use nuclear weapons.[12]

---

[12] For a study on this, see Jelnov, Tauman, and Zeckhauser, (2018).

This may be true while North Korea remains a risk-averse actor. But Kim's extensive provocations, efforts to expand nuclear weapon production and threaten the United States, and his fiery and aggressive threats suggest that he is increasingly a risk-taker. In addition, Kim seems more likely to consider war and nuclear weapon use in situations in which he feels desperate because of internal instability and threats, conditions in which he would almost certainly be a risk-taker. A RAND report titled *What Deters and Why* explains why strategic ambiguity is a weak alternative to strategic clarity in the current security environment and especially when facing a risk taker:

> *This analysis suggests that clarity in what is to be deterred, and how the United States will respond if deterrence fails* is the second essential element of a successful deterrent posture. Lack of clarity invites opportunistic aggression and provides fuel for wishful thinking for highly motivated aggressors; and there are no identifiable cases of failed extended deterrence in which the United States was entirely clear in its interests and intent. (Mazarr et al., 2018, p. xiii, emphasis added)

President Yoon is reportedly focused "on reassuring South Koreans that the country's defenses are sound" (Kim, 2023). He has apparently concluded that the U.S position of asking the ROK for relatively blind trust is no longer accomplishing ROK nuclear assurance. Specifically, President Yoon "has been pushing to have a say in the process of the U.S. planning and executing Washington's deterrence procedures, including the potential employment of nuclear arms" (Song, 2022b). President Yoon is looking for nuclear umbrella transparency and clarity. He presumably hopes that the Washington Declaration of April 2023 should be the means to gain that clarity (Lee H., 2023c).

Moreover, many ROK citizens want a guarantee from the United States that it will respond to North Korean nuclear weapon use with U.S. nuclear weapon use.[13] ROK military leaders understand that the U.S. threat against North Korean regime survival described previously is not unique to U.S. responses against North Korean nuclear weapon employment; the United

---

[13] ROK military officials, discussions with Bruce Bennett, 2016–2023.

States would also threaten North Korean regime survival if the North invaded the ROK using purely conventional weapons. The North might thus perceive that it would suffer no additional losses if it uses nuclear weapons as part of a ROK invasion as opposed to not using them. Although the very wording *nuclear umbrella* seems to promise a U.S. nuclear response to North Korean nuclear weapon use, no U.S. President has said so directly, and many U.S. personnel tell their Korean colleagues that there is no such guarantee: It is a U.S. presidential decision that they cannot predict. This U.S. strategic ambiguity might be a sufficient deterrent in peacetime but be insufficient if the North Korean regime becomes desperate and takes risks because of internal political challenges.[14] The ROK is unlikely to have strong nuclear assurance if U.S. deterrence of North Korean nuclear weapon use could be insufficient in a crisis. The ROK could also be subject to a U.S. President reneging on the nuclear umbrella, as many in the ROK fear Donald Trump might if elected President in 2024 because of his various statements downplaying the alliance, including his reported proposal to completely withdraw U.S. forces from the ROK (Choi, 2022a). Additionally, in recent years, North Korea has been far more aggressive in threatening to use nuclear weapons against the ROK than the Soviets and Russians have been in threatening the North Atlantic treaty Organization (NATO), even related to the Russian invasion of Ukraine. These threats come as a combination of the aggressive North Korean ballistic missile testing program, especially in 2022, and the direct threats of North Korean nuclear weapon attacks on the ROK and the United States. In particular, Kim's transition in 2022 from a nuclear weapon posture that was intended to be defensive to a posture that is now increasingly open to being offensive has raised serious ROK concerns (O'Carroll, 2022).

Will North Korean Intercontinental Ballistic Missiles Lead the United States to Abandon Its Nuclear Umbrella?

Many ROK citizens worry most about the North Korean ICBM buildup because they fear that it could cause the United States to abandon its nuclear

---

[14] ROK military officials, discussions with Bruce Bennett, 2013–2023.

umbrella.[15] They know that even one North Korean nuclear weapon detonating in a U.S. city would be a major disaster for the United States, let alone the potential North Korean objective of dozens of ICBMs each carrying multiple nuclear weapons to threaten the United States. ROK citizens have difficulty understanding why the United States does not seem to be putting any significant effort into deterring North Korea's ICBM development effort. The failure of the United States to act in support of its own security leaves many in the ROK puzzling about whether they can truly trust the United States to provide for ROK security.

During the Cold War, France had similar worries relative to the Soviet development of ICBM threats to the United States. Starting in the 1950s, NATO perceived that it probably could not stop a Soviet invasion of West Germany using only conventional weapons because of Soviet conventional force superiority. Therefore, the United States planned to use tactical nuclear weapons against the Soviet forces to stop their advance if, after a Soviet invasion, NATO conventional forces began to fail. Indeed, by the early 1970s, the United States deployed about 7,300 tactical nuclear weapons in Europe (Center for Arms Control and Non-Proliferation, 2021b). But as the French observed the growing Soviet strategic nuclear forces threatening the United States, they concluded that the United States would be unwilling to use tactical nuclear weapons to defend France and the other NATO countries in such a case because the Soviets would retaliate against U.S. cities. When U.S. President John F. Kennedy indicated that he wanted to convince the Soviets of the U.S. nuclear umbrella offered to the NATO countries, French President Charles de Gaulle asked Kennedy if he was "ready to trade New York for Paris" (U.S. Department of State, 1961). Skeptical of Kennedy's commitment, de Gaulle proceeded to build an independent French nuclear weapon force to deter a Soviet invasion of France, promising massive damage to the Soviet Union if the Soviets decided to invade France. President Yoon recently referred to this analogy of giving "up New York to protect Paris," calling it a comparable problem to the situation faced by the ROK (Kim, 2023).

---

[15] Indeed, as noted previously, North Korea apparently plans its ICBM development with that objective in mind. North Korea likely perceives that casting major doubts on the U.S. nuclear umbrella guarantee is also the key to decoupling the ROK-U.S. alliance.

Some argue today that most NATO countries trust U.S. extended deterrence and its nuclear umbrella despite a more serious Russian ICBM threat to the United States, so why should the ROK not? There are many key differences between NATO and the ROK. First, the United States has offered the NATO countries a considerable degree of strategic clarity relative to its nuclear umbrella that it has never offered the ROK, including explanations of U.S. nuclear planning against the Soviets and Russians, involvement in U.S. nuclear planning, and the eventual sharing of U.S. nuclear weapons.[16] The United States does not appear to have taken any of these actions with the ROK, although they are exactly the kinds of actions that President Yoon is asking for and appears to be hoping that the Washington Declaration will yield.[17]

Indeed, the United States has treated the defense of its NATO allies as being integral to the defense of the United States. This strategic clarity has helped build trust that the United States will indeed apply its nuclear umbrella in Europe despite the Russian ICBM threat. In contrast, the United States has not treated the defense of the ROK in the same manner. For example, as U.S. President, Trump went as far as regularly saying that North Korean short-range missile tests were "no problem" because they were not a threat to the United States (Gallo, 2019). However, those short-range missiles are clearly a threat to the ROK, and North Korea has said that it is preparing to have them to deliver nuclear weapons against ROK targets (Zwirko, 2022), suggesting a significant difference in U.S. and ROK threat perceptions and interests. Such statements undercut ROK nuclear assurance, which is already undermined by a lack of U.S. attention. For example, the ROK media noted that North Korea is mentioned only three times in the U.S. National Security Strategy (Kang, 2022).

---

[16] The United States and its NATO allies have for decades referred to *nuclear sharing* as a condition in which U.S. nuclear weapons are stored on allied military bases under the custody of a U.S. military security team. In wartime, the plan is for a representative of the host country and a U.S. representative to each insert a key to activate each of these nuclear weapons. The U.S. custody team would then turn them over to the host force for delivery against targets designated by NATO.

[17] President Yoon said, "The nuclear weapons belong to the U.S., but the planning, information sharing, exercises and training should be carried out jointly by South Korea and the U.S." (Lee H., 2023a).

The challenge for the ROK-U.S. alliance is to strengthen assurance that is faltering. Is the United States prepared to sacrifice American lives to protect the ROK? The various actions associated with the Washington Declaration should make the defense of the ROK more integral to the defense of the United States. But this issue also needs to be viewed from a U.S. perspective. For example, how would the ROK respond to a conflict between China and the United States? If the United States supported Taiwan against a Chinese invasion and China attacked the U.S. Kadena Air Base in Japan, can the United States expect that the ROK would join the conflict on the U.S. side? The Mutual Defense Treaty Between the United States and the Republic of Korea (1953) potentially mandates such ROK support. After 70 years of U.S. protection of the ROK, the ROK might not become integral to U.S. defense if the ROK is not clearly positive in addressing such questions.

Failure to Rein in the North Korean Nuclear Weapon Buildup

The ambiguity of the U.S. nuclear umbrella has also caused ROK trust issues relative to the buildup of the North Korean nuclear weapon threat. Does the nuclear umbrella apply to reining in this buildup? After all, "Assurance goes beyond effective deterrence as it requires the United States to foster and maintain a firm belief in its allies that it will come to their defense should deterrence fail" (Go, 2022). How can the ROK trust the United States to enter a likely destructive war on behalf of the ROK if the United States will not even make a serious effort in peacetime to rein in the buildup of North Korean nuclear weapons, weapon delivery means, and testing of those systems?

Potential Political Abandonment

The Trump presidency also raised concerns in the ROK about U.S. support. Trump downplayed the value of the ROK-U.S. alliance, terminated combined exercises that are key to the strength of the alliance, insisted that the ROK pay vastly more to help cover the costs of U.S. military support, and threatened to withdraw U.S. troops from the ROK (Gallo, 2021).[18] ROK fears were substantially amplified by the United States' withdrawal of its support from Afghanistan in 2021. Gallo (2021) wrote,

> Yet, the messy U.S. retreat from Afghanistan, and the ensuing Taliban takeover, has intensified questions here about how much South Korea should depend on long-term U.S. military protection and whether Seoul should do more to look after its own defense. Specifically, it may amplify voices who want South Korea to pursue its own nuclear deterrent.

ROK politics could also cause problems in the ROK-U.S. alliance. Although there is strong ROK support for the ROK-U.S. alliance today (Lee et al., 2023, p. 46), a new ROK president could weaken the alliance as one means for drawing closer to North Korea, presumably focusing on Korean Peninsula "peace" as a step toward Korean reconciliation. Such a president might refuse to participate in the kind of options designed to strengthen ROK nuclear assurance, as described in Chapters 3 through 6.

Although it is important to recognize that either U.S. or ROK politics could lead to undermining the ROK-U.S. alliance, both countries must decide that the alliance is important to them and avoid such confrontations.

Concern About the North Korean Nuclear Shadow

Even before Russia invaded Ukraine in February 2022, Russian President Vladimir Putin threatened "to retaliate harshly against any nations that intervened directly in the conflict" ("Ukraine Conflict Update: Feb 27, 2022," 2022). Four days after the invasion, he claimed that he put his nuclear forces on high alert in an apparent effort to deter outside intervention (Karmanau et al., 2022). This was a dramatic demonstration of the Russian *nuclear shadow*—the ability of a state with nuclear weapons to intimidate other states from responding strongly to its coercion or conventional attacks because the other states fear the potential for escalation into a nuclear war

---

[18] In fairness, the ROK president during much of President Trump's term pursued many policies opposed by the United States, raising questions in the United States about the utility of the ROK-U.S. alliance (O'Connor, 2021).

(Estes, 2020). The initial U.S. support to Ukraine was very small but gradually escalated, testing the Putin threat that was fortunately never executed.

Many worry that Kim Jong-un will become increasingly aggressive with his provocations and potentially even conventional attacks, believing that he can also cast such a nuclear shadow (Brewster, 2022). Indeed, North Korea might have already started doing so. Neither the United States nor the ROK responded very strongly to the North's tests of "at least 95 ballistic and other missiles" in 2022, apparently fearing North Korean escalation (Choe, 2023). And Kim has considerable incentives for carrying out provocations or limited attacks to demonstrate that, despite his many failings, he is still a powerful leader.[19] Kim faces considerable instability within North Korea; he is unable to feed his people, provide them with needed consumer goods, or sustain the availability of electrical power and other energy sources (Mun, 2022; Rengifo-Keller, 2023). Additionally, he has chosen to be brutally repressive even against his elites (O'Carroll and Chung, 2021).

What kind of aggression might Kim contemplate? He appears to be preparing for a seventh nuclear weapon test that, according to the discussion earlier in this chapter, could involve a 250 to 500 kt or larger explosion, which might give him broad international recognition and the appearance of success. His drone penetrations into the ROK in late December 2022 might have been a precursor of a drone swarm attack on important facilities in the ROK or ROK personnel (Bridley and Pastor, 2022). He could even decide that he can declare and enforce an alternative to the Northern Limit Line in the West Sea or conquer the ROK Northwest Islands. Kim might hope that, in taking any of these actions and others, his nuclear shadow would prevent any serious ROK-U.S. response. Thus, the continued North Korean nuclear weapon buildup affects not only the threat of North Korea launching a major war some years in the future but also the likelihood and potential severity of North Korean provocations and limited attacks in the short term as Kim tests his nuclear shadow, further undermining ROK nuclear assurance.

---

[19] Kim likely fears that if he becomes viewed as weak, he could face a coup.

China and Russia Preventing United Nations Action Against North Korea

For years, the United States was able to coordinate UN Security Council action against the most egregious of the North Korean nuclear weapon proliferation activities. Admittedly, the ROK and United States were forced on every occasion to scale back the measures that they wanted the Security Council to take against North Korea. China and Russia viewed these measures as too extreme. Still, UN Security Council resolutions against North Korea serve to both deny North Korea the resources it wants for its nuclear weapons programs and punish North Korea for the continued development of nuclear weapons and their delivery means that are prohibited by the UN Security Council. Since at least early 2022, China and Russia have refused to allow any UN Security Council resolutions against North Korea, taking away the principal means that had previously been used against the North Korean nuclear weapon program ("US Accuses Russia, China of Covering for North Korea at UN," 2023).

While the United States has taken some actions to fill this gap, its unilateral sanctions have not been very effective, and it has not chosen other responses of sufficient impact. In 2022, North Korea launched dozens of ballistic missile tests, including nearly a dozen ICBM tests, and yet the United States failed to apply a deterrence framework to prevent such tests or apply appropriate punishments in the aftermath of the tests. Although the United States did apply some sanctions against North Korean individuals and companies, it is important to note that North Korea almost never sends its agents overseas using their real names;[20] North Korea can thus change individual names and company names often, robbing such sanctions of significant impact. The United States might fear that more-serious actions against North Korea could lead to escalation, but the reality is that a failure to take any action has also resulted in the escalation of the North Korean nuclear weapon threat. In the absence of Chinese and Russian support in the UN Security Council, the United States could consider more-serious

---

[20] This statement is based on many interviews that Bruce Bennett has held with high-ranking individuals who escaped North Korea (North Korean escapees, discussions with Bruce Bennett, 2016–2023).

actions to rein in the North Korean nuclear weapon threat, as described in Chapter 3.

Other Issues That Challenge ROK Assurance

There appears to be no procedure for seeking ROK government approval, either in peacetime or during a conflict, for the use of U.S. nuclear weapons or even guidelines on what targets could be struck. This arrangement appears to differ from historical planning in NATO: "European NATO-allies were allowed to veto politically the use of those nuclear weapons that were under NATO command" (Berlin Information-Center for Transatlantic Security, 1997).[21] This is even more of a concern because, according to Article 3 of the ROK Constitution, "The territory of the Republic of Korea shall consist of the Korean peninsula and its adjacent islands" (ROK, 1987). Thus, technically, anywhere in North Korea that is targeted by U.S. nuclear weapons is ROK territory. The April 2023 Washington Declaration could lead to the needed procedures being developed ("Full Text of Washington Declaration Adopted at Yoon-Biden Summit," 2023).

Conclusion

Until the recent signing of the Washington Declaration, the U.S. government has appeared to have difficulty understanding the lack of ROK nuclear assurance. Indeed, the U.S. nuclear umbrella element of the U.S. extended deterrence commitment is a purposefully ambiguous strategy. As noted earlier, President Yoon has said, "'The so-called 'extended deterrence' also means that the U.S. will take care of everything, so South Korea should not worry'" (Choi and Kim, 2023). But U.S. action has been far more limited than this statement implies. In this chapter, we described how the current U.S. nuclear umbrella requires relatively blind ROK trust that adversary

---

[21] During the Cold War, the United States assigned some nuclear weapons under NATO for employment planning purposes. But those weapons could not have been used by NATO without explicit approval of the U.S. President.

and U.S. actions have jeopardized. The lack of strategic clarity of the U.S. nuclear umbrella is one challenge for the ROK that the Washington Declaration could help counter. But many in the ROK find the U.S. action also seriously lacking in several cases:

- North Korea has managed to develop a nuclear weapon force that appears to be an existential threat to the ROK, and U.S. efforts to forestall continued growth of that threat have been largely limited to economic measures that have not prevented that growth.
- North Korea seeks to deploy an ICBM force to threaten U.S. cities, apparently hoping to induce the United States to renege on its nuclear umbrella in the future. The United States has not done much to restrain those developments.
- The growing North Korean nuclear weapon force might increasingly allow the North to escalate its provocations and carry out limited attacks while fearing only restrained U.S. and ROK responses because of the North Korean nuclear shadow.

CHAPTER 3

Policy and Strategy Options

As North Korea's nuclear and missile capabilities have advanced by leaps and bounds since the early 2000s, many in the ROK perceive that the methods through which the United States has expressed its nuclear extended deterrence commitment have remained largely the same: an unelaborated reaffirmation of the U.S. defense commitment without context or details—essentially asking the ROK to exercise blind trust in an ambiguous U.S. commitment.[1] For many in the ROK public, such an outdated stance is epistemologically untenable in light of rapidly evolving North Korean threats and U.S. failure to contain the quantitative or qualitative growth in the North Korean nuclear weapon threat, as discussed in Chapter 2.

In this chapter, we describe options that the ROK and United States could exercise to strengthen ROK nuclear assurance, focusing on policy and strategy options. This is not an analytic process that argues for the higher utility of specific choices but rather a process of helping the ROK and U.S. people and their governments understand which options are available for dealing with the challenges of ROK nuclear assurance. Because North Korea actively threatens the ROK with nuclear weapon use and China does not, this chapter focuses on countering North Korean as opposed to Chinese nuclear weapon threats. The first options involve organizing the Nuclear Consultative Group (NCG) and providing education for both the ROK and U.S. national security communities on the nature of nuclear weapons, the damage they could cause, and what could be done to defend against

---

[1] This chapter was prepared by Bruce W. Bennett, Bruce E. Bechtol, Jr., and Myong-Hyun Go.

these weapons.[2] We then describe the major efforts that could reassure the ROK about U.S. extended deterrence (of which the nuclear umbrella is a part) using various options to achieve a strategy with more clarity. Finally, this chapter addresses options that could be exercised to rein in the North Korean nuclear weapon program. Although the ROK and United States had hoped to accomplish this objective through negotiations with the North, it now seems that a campaign of coercive measures could be needed to jump-start efforts to limit North Korean nuclear weapons. These measures are described from a strategy perspective, with more details on some specific options included in subsequent chapters.

Organizing the Nuclear Consultative Group

At the time of writing, the ROK and United States are working on organizing the NCG. We cannot predict how the NCG will eventually be organized. Nevertheless, that organization can make some difference in the level of ROK nuclear assurance. ROK citizens will likely pay attention to the level of national security leadership to which the NCG reports, the NCG working groups that are organized, and the frequency with which elements of the NCG meet. In particular, the NCG could report to the U.S. Secretary of Defense and the ROK Minister of National Defense, which could be achieved by having the NCG report to the ROK-U.S. security consultative meeting that those officials preside over.[3] The next level of NCG organization—effectively the chairman of the NCG—could be at the ROK Deputy Defense Minister of Policy and the U.S. Assistant Secretary of

---

[2] As part of the Washington Declaration, "[t]he two Presidents announced the establishment of a new Nuclear Consultative Group (NCG) to strengthen extended deterrence, discuss nuclear and strategic planning, and manage the threat to the nonproliferation regime posed by the Democratic People's Republic of Korea (DPRK)" ("Full Text of Washington Declaration Adopted at Yoon-Biden Summit," 2023).

[3] In a similar manner, the NATO Nuclear Planning Group "is chaired by the NATO Secretary General and generally meets at the level of defence ministers" (NATO, 2022b). Indeed, it can be expected that ROK security experts will compare the NCG with the Nuclear Planning Group and draw negative conclusions if the NCG does not play a similarly prominent role.

Defense for Indo-Pacific Security Affairs, the level at which much of ROK and U.S. national security policy is usually developed. Below these officials, working groups could be established to handle the various issues promised in the Washington Declaration. These working groups could focus on issues such as nuclear education, threat assessment, policy planning, and nuclear employment planning.

The NCG could be supported by the formation of a "team of strategic advisers" that was initially recommended by RAND and Asan (Bennett et al., 2021). This team of perhaps 15 to 20 ROK and U.S. nuclear weapon and national security experts could be tasked with providing the ROK and U.S. war planners, especially in the Combined Forces Command (CFC), with background understandings on nuclear weapons, their potential effects, and how they might be used by either side, and thus help organize the various tabletop exercises (TTXs) that the NCG is tasked with performing. The team likely would be derived from a combination of government personnel, academics, and military officers. Several of the U.S. participants should have experienced the NATO planning done during the Cold War to achieve *conventional-nuclear force integration*—the procedures for using conventional weapons and nuclear weapons in the same conflict area to achieve synergistic effects and avoid unwanted collateral damage. We expand on this proposed team in Chapter 4.

Preparing the ROK and United States: Education on Nuclear Weapon Issues

For both the ROK and the United States, most of their military and other national security personnel have little or no exposure to the effects of nuclear weapons and how to counter them. Because of the North Korean nuclear weapon threat described in Chapter 2, it is essential to provide these personnel with training on nuclear weapons. Doing so will help ROK national security personnel recognize the threat posed by North Korean nuclear weapon forces and what can be done about them; it will also demonstrate a U.S. understanding that something must be done about the North Korea nuclear weapon threat and that the United States is prepared to take such actions. The "team of strategic advisers" could provide a core group to help perform this training.

In practice, the training could involve two parts. The first would be basic instruction on the nature of nuclear weapons and their effects, which can be done with a variety of open-source material. This first part would also involve instruction on how to defend against North Korean nuclear weapons and be rather tactical in perspective. The second part of the training would focus on conventional-nuclear integration of military forces in a conflict and the specific threats that North Korea poses with its nuclear forces supporting its conventional forces. It would be more strategic and operational in perspective. For example, North Korea has regularly said that one of the objectives of its tactical nuclear weapons is to neutralize ROK military airfields. This training would explain the logic behind that North Korean threat and what might be done to sustain ROK and U.S. air force capabilities.

This education would not be a major contributor to ROK nuclear reassurance. But it would provide some reassurance and be potentially more important relative to convincing North Korea that the ROK is better prepared to deal with North Korean nuclear threats, strengthening deterrence.

Reassuring the ROK on U.S. Extended Deterrence

ROK nuclear assurance is fundamentally associated with its trust of the U.S. willingness and ability to exercise extended deterrence. As a first step, the ROK and United States have restarted their Extended Deterrence Strategy and Consultation Group (EDSCG), which had been suspended for more than four years, and are about to begin a NCG as part of the Washington Declaration (DoD, 2023b). Substantively, part of that trust requires the United States to clarify what it actually promises so that the United States' ability and willingness to exercise its nuclear umbrella can be assessed. That assessment is more likely to be positive if the U.S. nuclear umbrella is visible through demonstrable U.S. commitments to support the ROK with U.S. nuclear weapons, which we discuss in Chapter 5. Another aspect of that trust is associated with expanding the scope of U.S. nuclear umbrella efforts to include reining in the growth of the North Korean nuclear weapon threat and the hostility that the North displays, which we discuss in the next section. Note that, across the options described in this report, the team of strategic advisers introduced above could prove very useful.

Consulting on Deterrence Strategy

The EDSCG provides a forum for comprehensive discussions on strategy and policy issues to strengthen ROK-U.S. alliance deterrence on the Korean Peninsula and stability in the Indo-Pacific region.[4] A one-day meeting of this group involving the foreign affairs and defense agencies of the ROK and the United States was held in Washington, D.C., on September 16, 2022. A statement was issued at the close of this meeting, which said in part that

> [t]he United States reiterated its ironclad and unwavering commitment to draw on the full range of its military capabilities, including nuclear, conventional, missile defense, and other advanced non-nuclear capabilities, to provide extended deterrence for the ROK. The United States and the ROK made clear that any DPRK nuclear attack would be met with an overwhelming and decisive response. Both sides also confirmed their will to continue and strengthen close alliance consultation regarding U.S. nuclear and missile defense policy. (DoD, 2022a)

This was a strong statement of the solidarity of the U.S. and ROK alliance, but broader steps could be taken to improve the practical application of this statement and provide the ROK with more assurance of the robustness of the U.S. extended deterrence.

Moreover, this was only the third meeting of the EDSCG and the first since January 2018, a gap of more than four years. To be of greater value, the meetings could occur on a more regular basis. In addition, the meetings could move away from the generalities of joint statements after a one-day meeting and offer more specifics of how the United States intends to implement its extended deterrence. There are plans to hold working-level meetings of the EDSCG in the first part of 2023 (DoD, 2022a). The NCG could include task forces that work specific strategy issues.

---

[4] A history of this and related ROK-U.S. consultation efforts can be found in S. Choi (2023).

Strategy and Policy Options for Establishing Strategic Clarity

The United States has historically hoped that strategic ambiguity in its deterrent threats would achieve a maximum deterrent effect against adversaries. But, as noted in the discussion of the Healey Theorem in Chapter 1, ambiguity tends to undercut U.S. assurance of its allies (Yost, 2009). The declining trust in the U.S. extended deterrence in the ROK noted in Chapter 2 suggests that it is time to use more clarity for the benefit of U.S. key allies in Northeast Asia, particularly the ROK and Japan. Reassuring the ROK and Japan is a key aspect of maintaining stability in two alliances that are facing an often unpredictable and clearly dangerous threat—particularly because that threat includes nuclear weapons.

From the ROK perspective, the problem with the nuclear umbrella commitment is that there is no definition of its content or scope. An ironclad commitment to a vague promise is not much of a commitment. For example, if someone offered an ironclad offer to buy a home but refused to make a contract specifying the terms and conditions of the purchase, a seller would likely conclude that the prospective buyer's offer is not worth much. Has the buyer even determined that they have serious intent and the resources to make the purchase? When the United States offers an ironclad commitment to the conventional defense of the ROK, it has deployed conventional forces in the ROK, shared plans for deploying U.S. forces to the ROK, and made combined plans for that defense, suggesting that the U.S. conventional defense commitment is solid.

For the purposes of ROK nuclear assurance, the United States could add strategic clarity to the intent of the nuclear umbrella, including its scope and how the nuclear umbrella would be implemented. For example, is the U.S. nuclear umbrella offered to the ROK a U.S. commitment to use nuclear weapons in response to any North Korean nuclear weapon use? If the United States uses nuclear weapons, what objectives and effects would it seek to achieve? Does the United States also plan to handle all aspects of the North Korean nuclear weapon threat? If so, could the United States be doing more to rein in the growth in the North Korean nuclear weapon threat and the means that would be used to deliver those nuclear weapons? Should the United States also be attempting to rein in North Korean threats to employ nuclear weapons against the ROK? And if the United States does not plan to do so, is it leaving the ROK free to take such actions? One option for enhancing ROK nuclear assurance is for the United States to clearly answer these questions in ways designed to strengthen ROK security.

How Will the United States Respond to North Korean Nuclear Weapon Use?

Consider the first question about how the United States plans to respond to North Korean nuclear weapon use. U.S. officials have been consistent in arguing that U.S. extended deterrence for the ROK and the nuclear umbrella in particular are ironclad or rock-solid U.S. commitments. For example, in yearly meetings between high-level military and civilian officials from Washington and Seoul, the United States annually reaffirms its commitment to extended deterrence and the nuclear umbrella (Kim, 2021). This is important for the alliance because, if not clearly articulated, those in the ROK who have to worry about North Korea's nuclear weapons would be left in a very difficult position. The United States has never wavered from publicly announcing this position. In addition, after assuming the leadership of the ROK, President Yoon has made a major effort of strengthening the ROK-U.S. alliance. North Korean provocations and threats have contributed to the strengthened alliance, leading the ROK and United States to far more military cooperation and training.

By implication, the wording *U.S. nuclear umbrella* suggests that it ought to be a U.S. commitment to use its nuclear weapons whenever the ROK perceives a need for nuclear weapon employment so that the ROK does not need its own nuclear weapons. The United States has been very clear that a key component of the nuclear umbrella is sustaining ROK nuclear nonproliferation (Curtis E. Lemay Center, 2020). As noted in Chapter 2, consistent with this definition, many ROK national security experts want a U.S. commitment to use U.S. nuclear weapons in response to any North Korean nuclear weapon use; they think that the ROK would make such a deterrent threat if it had its own nuclear weapons.[5] They think that such an enhanced threat

---

[5]   We have heard this argument from dozens of conversations with senior ROK national security personnel, both military and civilian (ROK security personnel, discussions with authors, 2013–2018).

against North Korean nuclear weapon use is essential to deterrence because the ROK and United States have also threatened the survival of the North Korean regime if it ever invades the ROK, even with conventional weapons.[6] These experts think that, without a U.S. commitment to use nuclear weapons in response to North Korean nuclear weapon use, North Korea would conclude that there is no downside to using nuclear weapons once the North decides that it will invade the ROK. U.S. officials have apparently been reluctant to make this commitment because a decision to use nuclear weapons is reserved for the U.S. President, and they cannot predict such a decision.

U.S. officials have an easy option for responding to this ROK concern. Instead of taking the approach that the U.S. government cannot predict how a U.S. President would respond to North Korean use of nuclear weapons, the U.S. government could instead say that it anticipates that a U.S. President would use nuclear weapons in response to any North Korean use of nuclear weapons against the United States or its allies, which many in the ROK think should be the major essence of what a nuclear umbrella means. In practice, the current U.S. deterrent threat to North Korean regime survival does make such a commitment. If the North uses nuclear weapons, the regime will presumably have located itself in highly protected facilities, probably deep underground (see, for example, Moon, 2018): "Many of the more important strategic hard and deeply buried targets are beyond the

---

[6] As noted in Halloran (1998):

> To execute a decisive response, the Combined Forces Command that has operational control of U.S. and South Korean forces in South Korea is putting the finishing touches on a new war contingency plan. It calls on the military not only to repel a North Korean invasion but also to march north to demolish the North Korean armed forces and capture Pyongyang. A senior U.S. official in Seoul said that the North Korean regime would be ended and the country 'reorganized' under South Korean control.

This concept was not so new:

> South Korean state television said yesterday that Seoul and Washington have a plan to topple the North Korean government if the Stalinist state attacks the South. The Korean Broadcasting System said that rather than simply driving back the North's troops, the plan provides for a counteroffensive to seize Pyongyang and try to topple the government of Kim Il-sung. ("KBS Reports Plan to Topple Kim Il-sung," 1994)

As noted in Mann (1994), "the aim would be initially to contain North Korean forces north of Seoul, and then eventually launch a counterattack to defeat them there and overrun the rest of North Korea."

reach of conventional explosive penetrating weapons and can be held at risk of destruction only with nuclear weapons" (National Research Council of the National Academies, 2005). Thus a U.S. commitment to eliminate the North Korean regime is almost certainly a commitment to use U.S. nuclear weapons to achieve that destruction. Saying so explicitly, and especially by senior U.S. officials, would provide substance to the nuclear umbrella and could provide a significant degree of assurance to the ROK without pre-empting U.S. presidential prerogative.

Note, however, that there is a potential downside of strategic clarity: The United States might not be prepared to make the commitments associated with such clarity. For example, some future U.S. President could refuse to say anything at all about nuclear weapons or could even say that they never anticipates using nuclear weapons. Such a development would have severe consequences for both ROK nuclear assurance and deterrence of North Korea. Thus, before moving away from strategic ambiguity, it is critical that the U.S. President and their key personnel agree to the concept of strategic clarity and to what they mean by a nuclear umbrella. Otherwise, maintaining strategic ambiguity could be the best alternative for such a reluctant U.S. leadership.

Part of the problem is that the United States has chosen to refer to the nuclear umbrella as *rock solid* without defining what that umbrella is. In the future, U.S. officials might not have that alternative. Assume, for example, that North Korea decides to detonate a nuclear weapon at 50 km altitude over the East Sea 100 km east of Pohang, causing EMP damage to the southeastern part of the ROK. If that happens, many in the ROK will perceive that the U.S. nuclear umbrella has already failed because it did not deter North Korean nuclear weapon use or fulfill the other declared roles of U.S. nuclear weapons.[7] In this case, a U.S. President might not want to destroy the North Korean regime, feeling that, despite the U.S. deterrent threat in the Nuclear Posture Review to do so, regime destruction would not be a proportionate

---

[7] These roles are declared in the Nuclear Posture Review, which "affirms the following roles for U.S. nuclear weapons: Deter strategic attacks, assure allies and partners, and achieve U.S. objectives if deterrence fails" (DoD, 2022b, p. 7). If North Korea uses a nuclear weapon against the ROK, these first two roles have failed, leaving only one role remaining. In such a situation, what would be the U.S. objectives?

response and pose too high a risk of further escalation. Still, an appropriate U.S. limited nuclear weapon use could well reestablish nuclear deterrence and reassure the ROK. TTXs done under the promised NCG could address such cases to help the ROK and United States develop a strategy for such a situation, likely improve deterrence of North Korea, and strengthen ROK assurance and commitment to nuclear nonproliferation.

A Model for Establishing Strategic Clarity

A second step would be establishing a framework for how the United States would use its nuclear weapons against North Korea. In the late 1940s, the U.S. government put a shroud around its nuclear weapon program, eliminating allies from its nuclear weapon development efforts and denying allies information about U.S. nuclear weapons (Wampler, 1990). One result of doing so was a decision by the British and French governments to develop their own nuclear weapons.

By the early 1960s, the Soviet nuclear weapon threat was becoming very significant, especially against NATO. The United States worried that its NATO allies were not feeling nuclear assurance and that, unless it took more-proactive measures, more of its NATO allies would seek their own nuclear weapons. The United States did not want such nuclear proliferation: It had decided that preventing even its allies from developing nuclear weapons would be required to avoid broader global nuclear weapon proliferation that the United States feared would destabilize international security.[8] The United States therefore concluded that it needed to provide greater strategic clarity to reassure its NATO allies. The actions the United States took with its NATO allies provide useful options for ROK nuclear assurance.

In 1962, then–Secretary of Defense Robert McNamara outlined a series of actions that the United States was prepared to take in a speech to a NATO ministerial meeting in Athens. Few of these measures are being taken in Korea today, but some appear to be promised in the Washington Declaration. They included the following:

---

[8] The United States has this same attitude today and is against nuclear weapon development by any ally, including the ROK.

- The United States deployed 3,000 U.S. tactical nuclear weapons in Europe by 1960.[9] These nuclear weapons, combined with U.S. strategic nuclear weapons, gave the United States continuing superiority over the Soviet nuclear forces, providing strong deterrence against Soviet nuclear attacks. Even if the Soviets had pursued aggressive counterforce attacks against the forward deployed U.S. nuclear weapons, hundreds or more would have survived for use against the Soviet Union (McNamara, 1962, pp. 3, 5, 6).

- In the 1960s, the employment of Europe-based U.S. nuclear weapons was planned by the Supreme Allied Commander in Europe and his staff. These weapons would have been executed under his control once released by the U.S. President (McNamara, 1962, p. 5; Kristensen, 2005), allowing them to achieve tactical and operational effects in the theater, in addition to causing strategic damage.

- In addition to U.S. nuclear weapons deployed in Europe, a significant number of U.S.-based strategic nuclear weapons were committed to Soviet targets in Europe and targets in other countries that would have supported Soviet forces in Europe (McNamara, 1962, p. 5).

- The United States committed most of its ballistic missile submarine-based nuclear weapons to support NATO in the early 1960s (McNamara, 1962, p. 14).

- The United States provided its NATO allies with information on the numbers of each type of strategic nuclear weapon that the United States possessed and some future projections (McNamara, 1962, p. 4).

- The United States provided its NATO allies with aggregate information on the numbers of nuclear targets that were planned in Europe and the aggregate allocation of strategic and tactical nuclear weapons against them (McNamara, 1962, p. 5).

- McNamara committed to "a greater degree of alliance participation in formulating nuclear policies and consulting on the appropriate occasions for using these weapons" (1962, p. 6). In particular, McNamara spoke at the beginning of his presentation about involving NATO allies in "[t]he formulation of guidelines for the use of nuclear weap-

---

[9] The United States increased that number to a maximum of about 7,300 tactical nuclear weapons by 1971 (Norris and Kristensen, 2004).

ons" (1962, p. 1). This sounds very much like the role President Yoon sought in early 2023 and that was promised in the Washington Declaration.

A similar approach is presented in a study released in 2020:

> The U.S. nuclear umbrella, a legacy of decisions made in very different security environments in 1991 and 2010, is no longer fit for purpose as presently composed. It must be modified to enable improved signaling of collective resolve to stand up to North Korea's nuclear bullying. (Roberts, 2020)

The North Korean threat has significantly increased in recent years, but there have not been major changes to the extended deterrence commitment in recent years. Thus, in his conclusions, Roberts states that

> the United States should respond positively to rising calls in South Korea and Japan for more "NATO-like" extended nuclear deterrence in Northeast Asia. But they should resist simply importing the NATO model and instead adapt deterrence to the particular strategic context of contemporary Northeast Asia, while building on progress already made." (Roberts, 2020)

More generally, a former defense official, Zack Cooper, has stated publicly, "Although I think it would be a bad idea for South Korea to acquire nuclear weapons, the United States needs to do more to make sure that Seoul is comfortable with America's extended guarantees" (quoted in C. Lee, 2023).[10] Adjusting to the threat will be key as the ROK-U.S. alliance continues to make the moves necessary to defend the ROK from a North Korean nuclear attack. Potential policy and strategy options are described in the remainder of this chapter, with employment planning and execution options described in Chapter 4 and nuclear weapon force options discussed in Chapter 5.

---

[10] Zack Cooper was an official during the George W. Bush administration.

Identifying Available U.S. Nuclear Forces

The United States could provide the ROK with some specifics on the nuclear weapons currently in U.S. inventory, both those intended for theater use and those intended for strategic nuclear use. This information could include the types of nuclear weapons that the United States has available, the nature of their delivery means, and the numbers of such weapons, much like the information McNamara provided in his Athens speech. The United States could also provide basic information on the anticipated yield of these nuclear weapons, the operating characteristics of the delivery systems (for example, how many ballistic missile submarines carrying nuclear weapons are usually operating at sea in the Pacific?), and their anticipated performance. Historically, the United States was reluctant to divulge such information, hoping to avoid adversary understanding of the U.S. nuclear forces and how they could be attacked or otherwise defeated. In practice, the United States may already be making some such disclosures to the ROK (Song, 2022a). Today, much of this information is available on an open basis on the internet for those who go searching (see, for example, Nuclear Weapon Archive, 2023). Broader public awareness of some general parameters would likely strengthen ROK nuclear assurance.

How the United States Would Use Nuclear Weapons Against North Korea

Senior national security leaders in the ROK government could also be given information on any preplanned nuclear attacks on North Korea, including the numbers of nuclear weapon targets that the United States plans to strike in and the aggregate allocation of U.S. nuclear weapons against them. This information could also be categorized by type of target, and the ROK government could review and respond to these aggregate nuclear weapon employment plans. We expand on this discussion in Chapter 4.

Reining In the North Korea Nuclear Weapon Program

For 30 years, the ROK and U.S. governments have hoped to resolve the North Korean nuclear weapon threat to the ROK by negotiating the denuclearization of North Korea. The United States speaks regularly about being willing to meet with the North Korean government anytime and anywhere to discuss North Korean denuclearization (Lee and Kim, 2022). But North Korea refuses to negotiate and has repeatedly said that it will never denuclearize (D. Choi, 2022b; T. Kim, 2022). Full denuclearization is not the only option. Because North Korea appears to be continually producing more nuclear weapons, the ROK and United States could seek a partial or full North Korean nuclear weapon production freeze: The future would be better for the ROK and United States if North Korea has only its current 50 to 100 nuclear weapons rather than the 300 to 500 Kim Jong-un appears to be seeking. We therefore consider an effort to coerce North Korea into a nuclear weapon production freeze (i.e., Kim would stop his nuclear weapon production, while giving up no existing weapons) as an initial step in reining in the North Korean nuclear weapon program.[11]

Why is this important? It is generally recognized that North Korea is a revisionist regime that seeks to achieve some level of peninsula dominance to allow it to have control of the fate of the Korean people (see, for example, Bennett et al., 2021, pp. 2–3, p. 9; and Hwang, 2022, p. 518), and it also seeks revenge against the United States.[12] Thus, anything that can be done to limit the North Korean nuclear weapon buildup reduces the threats to the ROK and United States.

---

[11] Such a North Korean nuclear weapon freeze would not meet the ROK-U.S. long-stated demand for North Korean denuclearization. A North Korean nuclear weapon freeze would thus not be an end state but a pragmatic first step that is required to eventually achieve North Korean denuclearization.

[12] North Korean strategic culture can be characterized by the following messages: "The threats of imperialism are overwhelming, and Korea is always surrounded by them. It is a sacred duty to seek revenge, as the lives of the invaded people are miserable. Nevertheless, imperialism will eventually fall and the triumph of history is destined" (Hwang, 2022, p. 518).

Alternatives to Negotiation

Simple negotiation is not the only option for the ROK and United States to try to rein in the developing North Korean nuclear weapon threat. Although the ROK and United States would prefer to rein in this threat in cooperation with the North, they could also attempt to do so using coercive measures. With coercive measures, the ROK and United States would tell North Korea what they want the North to do and threaten to take specific actions against North Korea if the North refuses to rein in its nuclear weapon buildup. For example, the United States could threaten to forward base a U.S. aircraft carrier in Busan if North Korea continues its ballistic missile tests. Such threats could become more powerful against North Korea if they were also against the interests of China, giving China reason to pressure North Korea to accede to ROK and U.S. demands. For example, the ROK could threaten to join the U.S. missile defense system if North Korea continues its ballistic missile tests, which might anger the Chinese leadership. Of course, there is no guarantee that North Korea will follow these ROK-U.S. demands. Thus, the ROK and United States must be prepared to follow through on their threats if North Korea continues its aberrant behavior. A failure to follow through would undermine any subsequent coercive measures. The ROK and United States must also be prepared for escalatory actions by North Korea and potentially China in response to these coercive measures. They must be prepared to deal with such escalations and be thinking three or more moves ahead.

The U.S. government organizes its options for action (including coercive measures) into four categories reflected in the acronym DIME: diplomatic, information, military, and economic. As noted previously, for years the ROK and United States primarily pursued the diplomatic option, hoping to avoid any risk of escalation or retaliation. In the process, the ROK and United States worked with the UN to implement economic sanctions in response to mainly North Korean nuclear weapon tests. These sanctions have significantly hurt the North Korean economy, but North Korea's closing of its borders to the outside world, an action that the North has argued was necessary because of the coronavirus disease 2019 (COVID-19) pandemic, has also significantly hurt the North Korean economy. Meanwhile, North Korea has refused to continue diplomatic efforts. Indeed, Kim has argued that he is unwilling to denuclearize (RFA Korean, 2022). In the ROK, most people perceive denuclearization as no longer possible (Nam K., 2022).

Thus, although the ROK and United States continue to offer diplomacy to North Korea, we examine options for ROK and United States action in the other three DIME categories. Like the options discussed previously, the NCG could play a primary role in formulating the required coercive program, assisted by the proposed team of strategic advisers.

Economic Measures

North Korean development of nuclear weapons and the platforms that carry these weapons to their targets is a very expensive endeavor. Although the UN, the United States, the ROK, and other nations have applied a variety of economic sanctions on North Korea, the North has chosen to have its people suffer so that it can continue its work on nuclear weapons and their delivery means.

Indeed, it often puzzles those who do not follow North Korea closely that Pyongyang is able to fund these expensive nuclear and missile programs given that the North's gross domestic product is only about $40 billion per year (U.S. Central Intelligence Agency, 2023). It is worth describing how North Korea raises money to maintain and improve its military capabilities. The main answer is illicit activities. Probably 40 percent of North Korea's real economy comes from illicit activities, such as military proliferation, sales of illegal drugs, and cyber theft, and a senior U.S. official reported that half of the funding for just the North's missile development comes from illicit cyber activities (Ponnudurai, 2013; Reddy, 2023b). The funds that North Korea raises from these activities (in the billions of dollars each year) have to be laundered somewhere.

The key U.S. economic action is to sanction the third parties that North Korea uses to support the funding and provision of materials for its nuclear weapon program, including phony front companies in key countries, such as Singapore and Malaysia, and banks in African countries, Iran, the United Arab Emirates, and China that launder the money North Korea has gleaned from illicit activities (Choy, 2020; Pearson and Latiff, 2017). The way to go after these funds and squeeze North Korea is to use secondary sanctions against the third parties, but the U.S. government has been hesitant over several presidential administrations to fully implement these sanctions for fear of third-party retaliation.[13] Enhanced enforcement of existing, available sanctions would allow the United States to sanction or at least fine banks that look the other way as North Koreans deposit their money. These banks often exist in China or Russia (Hsu, 2019). Unless banks in these countries are sanctioned or fined, the existing sanctions have no real effect. Similarly, North Korean front companies in countries that are friendly to the United States could be shut down, and further monitoring could occur so new ones are promptly handled. Companies in places such as Russia that are detected selling materials to North Korea that are used in Pyongyang's weapons of mass destruction programs could be sanctioned, but, just as importantly, these sanctions could be more strongly enforced.[14]

It is already difficult for North Korea to get around sanctions, and sanctions relief is likely to be one of the first things—if not the first thing— pushed for if negotiations occur again. Thus, containing North Korea's illegal and illicit financial networks will put real pressure on the Kim Family Regime—and will also likely cause it to engage in more-provocative behavior. This behavior could be seen as a disadvantage, yet to not act (or to put a fine point on it, to continue to not take sufficient action to put pressure on North Korea's financial networks) means North Korea will continue to fund its expensive nuclear weapon programs relatively unabated.

Military Measures

Although military attacks by the United States or ROK on the North could destroy many of its nuclear weapon–related production and test facilities,

---

[13] As noted in Bartlett and Ophel (2021), "[S]econdary sanctions present non-U.S. targets with a choice: do business with the United States or with the sanctioned target [North Korea], but not both." Thus, Chinese companies that contravene UN sanctions by buying more than the allowed amount of North Korean coal could be told that if they continue doing such business with North Korea, they will not be allowed to do any business with the United States.

[14] For an excellent example of the United States sanctioning North Koreans and foreign companies (e.g., Russian companies) that are helping use illicit finances and illegal trade practices to support North Korean weapons of mass destruction development, see U.S. Department of the Treasury (2022).

such action would almost certainly lead to war with North Korea. The ROK and United States appear to be so anxious to avoid such a war that it is difficult to imagine either taking chances with military attacks. Some military measures are being used and could be enhanced, and others could be added. Possibilities include the following:

1. The ROK and United States could threaten to continue increasing the numbers and sophistication ROK-U.S. military exercises on peninsula. The ROK and United States have been doing this, but they could threaten to increase these activities further if North Korea fails to restrain its nuclear weapon–related programs.

2. The United States could similarly threaten more-regular deployments of U.S. strategic weapon systems (e.g., bombers, aircraft carriers, nuclear submarines) to the peninsula (see Chapter 5 for further discussion of this possibility).

3. The ROK could threaten to join the U.S.-led ballistic missile defense system.[15]

4. The ROK and United States could threaten to take coercive actions associated with ROK nuclear assurance against North Korea if it does not rein in its military tests or nuclear weapon and missile production. Potential coercive actions could include threatening to deploy U.S. tactical nuclear weapons in the ROK (as discussed in Chapter 5).

5. The ROK and United States could threaten to create a formal trilateral alliance that includes Japan against both North Korea and China. The trilateral U.S., ROK, and Japan summit in August 2023 was a first step in this direction (White House, 2023). As part of this alliance relationship, the three allies could coordinate their plans (e.g., the ROK kill chain, the Japanese counterstrike capability) for striking North Korean threats (Bennett, 2022b).

6. The United States could threaten to deploy in the ROK the U.S. hypersonic missiles that are currently under development.

---

[15] For more information on the ROK's ballistic missile defense capabilities and its decision not to join the U.S.-led ballistic missile defense system, see Missile Defense Advocacy Alliance (2022).

In each case, the ROK and United States could threaten a specific consequence to North Korea (and China) if the North continues some specific element of its nuclear weapon and delivery system production or testing.

There are other key actions that have been taken that deterred North Korea's provocations. For example, the U.S. Space Force established its first unit on foreign soil in the ROK. According to U.S. Forces Korea, the unit "will be tasked with coordinating space operations and services such as missile warning, position navigation and timing and satellite communications within the region," which will not be welcomed by North Korea (Lendon and Bae, 2023).

Information Measures

The ROK and United States could alternatively use information to coerce North Korea and rein in the North Korean nuclear weapon threat. For example, South Korean music, movies, and dramas are winning the hearts of young North Koreans. This media influence is seen as a threat to Kim's grip on society. Kim has made it clear that he is very fearful of such outside information, even decrying K-pop music as a "vicious cancer" that is corrupting the culture of the younger generation (Choe, 2021). North Korean media has argued that, unless North Korean exposure to K-pop is brought under control, K-pop could cause the regime to "crumble like a damp wall" (Choe, 2021)—the most fearful threat to Kim. Indeed, the North has effectively declared a war against outside information, although it is a war that the North is not winning (S. Lee, 2023).

The ROK and United States could also use a variety of other kinds of information. For example, they could send information into North Korea saying that the famine conditions in the North could be resolved by purchasing outside food in exchange for a small reduction in what the regime is spending on its nuclear weapons.[16] For delivery to the elites in Pyongyang,

---

[16] There apparently is already some discontent in the North relative to inadequate food:

> North Koreans are reportedly expressing discontent about the continuous shows of force this year, complaining that they do not know what they will do with the authorities firing off missiles while rice prices climb due to the protracted COVID-19 pandemic and law enforcement crackdowns prevent them from making a daily living. (C. Lee, 2022a)

an information operation could talk about the reasons that Kim Jong-un closed North Korea's borders to the outside world, ostensibly to protect the North from COVID-19. However, it was likely more important to Kim to significantly reduce the flow of outside information into the North and bankrupt many of the North Korean entrepreneurs who had become wealthy via trade with China and could thus avoid having to do as directed by the regime by bribing officials. More seriously, the ROK and United States could regularly commend Kim for his extreme provocations and rhetoric, as Kim's behavior has made the ROK-U.S. alliance probably closer than ever. For a regime anxious to decouple the ROK-U.S. alliance, the North has actually achieved the opposite effect, which would reflect and highlight Kim's lack of understanding of the outside world.

Managing North Korean Retaliation and Escalation

In the past few years, North Korea has shown a significant propensity to retaliate against ROK-U.S. defensive activities. In practice, North Korea pursues its own coercive measures by, for example, seeking to get the ROK and United States to abandon their military exercises by carrying out extensive missile tests. When the ROK and United States threaten coercive measures against North Korea, North Korean countermeasures, likely escalation, and engagement in more-provocative behavior should be expected. Managing this escalation can be done by threatening not only immediate consequences to stop the undesired North Korean behavior but also subsequent consequences if North Korea (or China) chooses to escalate. Note also that such coercive measures should likely not be done publicly because doing so would give Kim strong incentives to escalate in response; he would not want to appear to be willing to surrender to U.S. coercion and thereby look weak. Instead, these coercive measures are best used privately, perhaps through the North's office at the UN, which would allow Kim to avoid appearing weak.

For example, the United States does not want a North Korean ICBM test on a normal trajectory over the Pacific. Not only would such a test give North Korea confidence in its ICBMs and coercive power with them, but a risk-taking North might also claim to be doing a nuclear weapon test on such a launch and have that "test" designed to cause major EMP damage to Hawaii or the West Coast of the United States. The United States could thus threaten to shoot down such an ICBM after it is launched, denying the North confidence in its performance and preventing a potential EMP attack (Bennett, 2023). In response, the North might threaten to conduct a seventh nuclear weapon test. The ROK and United States could threaten North Korea that if it conducts this test, they will send 1 million USB drives into the Pyongyang area (to the elite) with K-pop, K-dramas, and other messages (Bennett, 2022a). When threatening North Korea, the ROK and United States could also tell the North that their next escalatory threat would be building nuclear weapon storage facilities at airfields in the ROK to facilitate rapid deployment of U.S. nuclear weapons to the ROK (see Chapter 5 for further discussion). The ROK and United States could also privately inform China about these coercive measures, which China would not want, allowing China to attempt to restrain the North. The United States could also remind North Korea that the United States will not allow the regime to survive if it uses a nuclear weapon and inform the North that launching a nuclear weapon for a test on a ballistic missile would be considered using a nuclear weapon.

There is no public information suggesting that the United States has taken such coercive measures to rein in the North Korean nuclear weapon and ballistic missile program. If the United States had done so, one would have expected that the United States would have especially sought to deter North Korean ICBM tests. The United States would be more secure if the North had not been able to test its ICBMs to the point that they perceive that these missiles would work; the United States could therefore have been motivated to take coercive measures against this testing. But after perhaps a dozen North Korean ICBM-related tests since early 2022, and no open major U.S. responses to any of them, it seems likely that the United States has not applied coercive measures against the North's ICBM-related tests. Presumably the United States has feared North Korean escalation and assumed that a lack of ROK nuclear assurance is not such a serious threat that it justifies escalation risks with the North.

Admittedly, coercive measures do pose some potentially significant risks. But would applying these measures now be any riskier than having to deal with North Korea's coercive measures when it has 300 or so nuclear weapons and 50 ICBMs for delivering nuclear weapons?

CHAPTER 4

Employment Planning and Execution Assurance Options

In this chapter, we transition from examining broad ROK-U.S. strategy and policy to assessing options for strengthening ROK nuclear assurance through enhancing ROK-U.S. planning and operations.[1] Because North Korea actively threatens the ROK with nuclear weapon use and China does not, this chapter focuses on countering North Korean nuclear weapon threats. The assurance options consist of developing a ROK-U.S. common threat description, enhancing ROK-U.S. conventional military force capabilities, preparing for nuclear warfighting, involving the ROK government in approving nuclear employment planning, and strengthening trilateral ROK-U.S.-Japan cooperation. Note that we describe these options rather than analyzing the relative utility of each.

Developing a Common View of the North Korean Threat

The first step in developing any ROK-U.S. military plans is to create a common view of the North Korean threat. Because of the threats discussed in Chapter 2, especially the recent North Korean threats of offensive, countermilitary nuclear weapon use, this common view of the North Korean threat must include potential North Korean nuclear weapon use. We propose that two products be prepared: (1) a sensitive ROK-U.S. government

---

[1] This chapter was prepared by Gregory S. Jones, Du-Hyeogn Cha, and Bruce W. Bennett.

threat estimate that will be used as the basis for detailed operations planning and (2) an openly available ROK-U.S. threat assessment that would allow the ROK and U.S. citizens to understand the dangers that North Korea is posing. An NCG threat assessment working group could take the lead in preparing these products.

Historically, the United States has openly published several North Korean threat assessments that focused on potential North Korea invasions of the ROK (see, for example, Army Techniques Publication 7-100.2, 2020; U.S. Marine Corps Intelligence Activity, 1997) but has said much less about potential North Korean limited or coercive attacks and almost nothing about the potential impact of North Korean nuclear weapons used as part of limited or major warfare. The ROK has also not comprehensively analyzed how the North Korean nuclear weapon issue could affect conflict on the Korean Peninsula. For this reason, creating these assessments would help both countries better understand the North Korean nuclear weapon threats. Moreover, these assessments could address North Korea's nuclear weapon threats beyond the Korean Peninsula and examine potential reactions of neighboring countries to North Korean nuclear weapon use and potential ROK-U.S. responses. These efforts could also assess the Chinese nuclear weapon threats.

Improving the Nonnuclear Force Balance, Countering the North's Nuclear Shadow

A 2020 ROK poll showed that a plurality of respondents viewed North Korea as being militarily superior to the ROK (Lee et al., 2020, p. 20). This perception was likely seriously affected by the North Korean nuclear weapon forces. A more recent poll indicates that 57 percent of those surveyed found ROK conventional forces superior to those of the North (versus 18 percent who felt the reverse). However, when nuclear weapons are included, a significant plurality found North Korea to be stronger than the ROK (Lee et al., 2023, pp. 56–58). There does not appear to be much perception in the ROK that the North poses a conventional-force invasion threat in the next few years, most likely because many North Korean weapon systems are very old. However, even if North Korea could not successfully invade the ROK, its conventional forces might still cause significant damage, even with limited attacks. The late-2022 incursions by North Korean drones suggests one possibility for a North Korean limited attack (Song, 2022c). Therefore, the ROK and United States could enhance their nonnuclear military force capabilities, giving them depth, advanced technology, and diversity of those capabilities for deterring North Korean provocations, especially limited attacks, thereby reducing North Korean incentives to carry out limited attacks on the ROK. This deterrence could significantly enhance ROK assurance.

But several changes in potential ROK military power jeopardize the current balance. The most serious is the North's nuclear weapon threat, especially to the ROK Air Force. Another important factor is the declining size of the ROK Army. ROK demographics have reduced the size of the ROK military forces, and those reductions have all been made in the ROK Army. In an attempt to trade manpower for technology, the ROK has particularly focused on creating very powerful conventional air forces that could disrupt any North Korean Army attack on the ROK (Bennett, 2006). North Korea's recent focus on using nuclear weapons to neutralize ROK air bases clearly targets this ROK development.

There are options for the ROK and United States to respond to these challenges. Both can counter the North's nuclear threat to ROK air bases by enhancing defenses against nuclear weapon attacks on those bases, including providing dispersal bases, enhancing the layers and depth of ROK missile and air defense, otherwise enhancing the ROK three-axis system, and enhancing defenses against North Korean special forces and similar threats (Bennett, 2020, p. 283; Bowers and Hiim, 2021).[2] The declining size of the ROK Army can be dealt with in part by creating a two-tier army reserve system and enhancing investments in advanced army weapon systems (Bennett, 2006, pp. 275–276). Both can be improved by strengthening the ROK-U.S. alliance to provide more-visible U.S. support to ROK nonnuclear forces and by providing more and greater joint military planning and exercise efforts. All these actions will require greater budgets for the ROK Ministry of National Defense.

---

[2] The ROK Air Force could consider using part of its reserve personnel to enhance ROK Army protections against North Korean personnel attacking ROK air bases.

Kim is mounting a particular effort to stop or at least limit ROK-U.S. military exercises.[3] This is part of his effort to decouple the ROK-U.S. alliance because combined military exercises are key to the health of the ROK-U.S. alliance. If North Korea can eliminate or significantly reduce the exercises and training, it will weaken alliance effectiveness and cooperation. And if the alliance becomes less effective and demonstrates lower cooperation, ROK public opinion could perceive that the United States lacks the capability and will to support ROK security. Ultimately, if such public opinion develops, U.S. forces in the ROK could also be drastically reduced or withdrawn. This dynamic is why North Korea claims that ROK-U.S. exercises will increase tensions on the Korean Peninsula. The ROK and United States could make more effort to explain why combined ROK and U.S. military exercises are useful and effective.

Actions to enhance the nonnuclear force balance could strengthen deterrence of North Korean aggression and confidence in U.S. extended deterrence commitments. Of particular concern is that North Korea appears to be increasingly feeling the leverage that its nuclear shadow gives for carrying out provocations with conventional forces. The ROK ability to deter such provocations by denial (reducing the likelihood that they would be effective) could make a significant contribution to ROK assurance. And the ROK could undermine any perception by Kim that he can successfully execute a major attack on the ROK.

However, there could also be various disadvantages of these actions. The paranoia of Kim would likely be enhanced because he fears ROK-U.S. efforts to build sufficient conventional-force superiority to invade and defeat North Korean forces. The growing ROK three-axis system, which consists of all nonnuclear capabilities, could be destabilizing in crises, as discussed in later sections. These conventional capabilities will also be expensive and divert investments from ROK domestic programs or other military capabilities.

---

[3] See how North Korea is trying to constrain ongoing ROK-U.S. military exercises in Shin (2023a).

Creating Defenses Against North Korean Nuclear Weapon Use

Because North Korea is actively threatening nuclear weapon attacks against the ROK and United States, the ROK and United States could adjust their deterrence and warfare planning to counter North Korean nuclear weapon threats and attacks. For example, even if North Korea planned to carry out limited attacks on the ROK using only conventional weapons, North Korea would most likely threaten any ROK-U.S. responses with nuclear escalation, similar to what Russia has done in its war against Ukraine.

ROK and U.S. efforts to counter North Korean nuclear weapon use could be made in several increments. First, the basic education on nuclear weapon issues discussed in Chapter 3 could proceed. Second, the North Korean threat could be better depicted. Then the ROK and United States could build a more comprehensive defense framework to protect the ROK from North Korean nuclear weapon attacks. This framework would include the existing ROK and U.S. capabilities. CFC could then transition to working on nuclear warfighting, which is discussed in the following section.

These tasks will require support from individuals who have worked on nuclear weapon employment and particularly conventional-nuclear weapon integration. The team of strategic advisers introduced in Chapter 3 could provide this expertise.

Active Defense Against North Korean Nuclear Attacks

Active defense involves employing "offensive action and counterattacks" against adversary attacks (DoD, 2021, p. 7). The ROK has already been pursuing active defense capabilities to counter North Korean attacks that could involve nuclear weapons. It has prepared a three-axis system and is now considering adding a kill web capability to employ nonkinetic offensive means and make the three-axis system more effective (Song and Chae, 2023). The three-axis system consists of three components: the Kill Chain strike system, the Korea Air and Missile Defense system, and Korea Massive Punishment and Retaliation. These three components are intended to work together but can operate separately and have value as stand-alone systems. Therefore, we examine them separately. The *kill web* is a new concept of the Yoon administration. These capabilities strengthen both deterrence of North Korea and the ROK and U.S. ability to prevail if deterrence fails, significantly contributing to ROK nuclear assurance.

The Kill Chain Strike System

The Kill Chain is a system that can carry out strikes against North Korea's nuclear and missile facilities and weapons. This system has been under development since at least 2011.[4] In addition, the United States apparently plans to execute counterforce attacks against North Korea with similar operational concepts and capabilities. In any conflict, CFC can be expected to use both the ROK kill chain and U.S. counterforce capabilities. Both countries employ reconnaissance capabilities to locate North Korean nuclear weapons and their delivery systems and apparently share some of that information. The ROK relies primarily on its Hyunmoo ballistic missiles for striking targets in North Korea; the United States relies primarily on fighter aircraft and drones. All these weapons can be very accurate, with the Hyunmoo-2C having a circular error probable of 1 to 5 m (Missile Defense Project, 2021b).[5]

The ROK and United States could be enhancing and integrating the ROK kill chain system and U.S. counterforce strikes. Although such attacks on North Korea might be difficult to carry out preemptively, they do not need to be preemptive to have an impact because North Korea will not launch all its missiles in a first strike (Green, 2013). The North has multiple missiles for each launcher and is expected to try to retain a significant strategic reserve force (Bennett, 2022b). Thus, targeting North Korean nuclear weapons and their delivery means after a North Korean surprise first strike in a war could ease the burden on ROK and U.S. missile defense systems and reduce at least some of the massive damage that these nuclear strikes might otherwise cause.

---

[4] ROK national security official, interview with Bruce Bennett, 2011.

[5] *Circular error probable* is a measure of a delivery system's accuracy. It is the radius of a circle inside of which one-half of all shots should land.

Korean Air and Missile Defense System and Other Active Defenses

North Korean nuclear attacks against the ROK will very likely be conducted by ballistic missiles, cruise missiles, or aircraft. Intercepting these attacking missiles or aircraft will be one means of protecting the ROK. The ROK and United States have already made significant investments in air and missile defenses. The ROK uses Patriot missile defenses and fighter aircraft, has acquired SM-2 missiles and is acquiring SM-3 and SM-6 missiles for its warships (Chae, 2023), and is developing long-range SAM and medium-range SAM land-based missile defense systems (GlobalSecurity. org, 2022). The United States has deployed Patriot and THAAD air and missile defenses in the ROK, has fighter aircraft, and has warships available with SM-2, SM-3 and SM-6 capabilities. The United States also has satellites to cue missile defenses. The ROK, United States, and Japan have agreed to share missile-tracking data that should enhance interceptor performance (Takemoto and Kaneko, 2023).

ROK and U.S. efforts to enhance these defenses is one option for strengthening ROK nuclear assurance. Such efforts are already ongoing, including completing the existing THAAD battery and some discussion of follow-on THAAD batteries (Yoon, 2021).[6] These air and missile defenses can directly protect ROK cities from attack by nuclear-armed North Korean missiles. Such protection is more difficult, although not impossible, for Seoul because of its proximity to North Korea. But protecting military installations and ROK cities further south could provide significant deterrence and defense against North Korean nuclear attacks. For example, using Patriot interceptors to protect airfields, such as the Osan Air Base, would make it much

---

[6] For the U.S. Army, which operates THAAD, personnel often deploy to Korea without their families. Because many Army personnel are married, this is a hardship that the Army tries to lessen by limiting deployments to about one out of every three years. With such a rotation schedule, the seven U.S. Army THAAD batteries are already stretched by deployments in the ROK, Guam, and the Persian Gulf (McCall, 2022). An eighth THAAD battery is not expected to be delivered until fiscal year 2025 ("Missile Defense Agency Officials Hold a Press Briefing on President Biden's Fiscal 2024 Missile Defense Budget," 2023). It is thus unlikely that the United States could provide another THAAD battery for deployment to the ROK. But the ROK could purchase a THAAD battery and forgo the personnel rotations required by the United States.

more difficult for Kim to achieve his objective of neutralizing such air bases, even with nuclear weapons. Air and missile defenses could also protect U.S. tactical nuclear weapons deployed in the ROK should such an option be exercised, helping these weapons survive an initial North Korean nuclear attack so that they could be used to strike back.[7]

China has been an impediment to enhancing ROK and U.S. missile defenses. China carried out economic warfare against the original THAAD battery deployment and now demands that the ROK limit other such deployments (Fretwell, 2022). When North Korea claimed that its missile tests were practice for attacks on the ROK (Kim and Smith, 2022), President Yoon asked Chinese President Xi Jinping to help rein in North Korea's provocations, but Xi refused (Nam H., 2022).

As noted in Chapter 2, North Korean ICBMs are also a concern. The United States has built its Ground-Based Midcourse Defense (GMD) to protect the U.S. homeland from North Korean ICBM attack. GMD is an essential element of the U.S. missile defeat approach, and there are plans for its modernization and expansion (DoD, 2022a). Options for strengthening ROK assurance with U.S. homeland missile defense include periodic testing of the GMD system to demonstrate its ability to intercept targets, such as North Korean ICBMs, integration with the U.S. Navy's SM-3 ship-based interceptors, and accelerated qualitative improvements for the GMD system to keep up with the growing North Korean threat.

North Korea's Massive Punishment and Retaliation

The first two parts of the three-axis defense system involve trying to limit the damage that North Korean nuclear weapons could inflict on the ROK or the United States. Korea Massive Punishment and Retaliation is a mix of deterrence and punishment and seeks to disconnect the North Korean leadership to prevent nuclear weapon launches while punishing the North Korean leaders by eliminating them if they do use nuclear weapons. Because Kim is most concerned with his own survival and continued control of North Korea, this is a very powerful deterrent threat to prevent major North Korean aggression. To make the threat more powerful by extending it to the North Korean

---

[7] Currently, the United States possesses only aircraft-delivered tactical nuclear weapons, which is discussed in more detail in Chapter 5.

elites more broadly, the ROK threatened a massive attack that would turn "[e]very Pyongyang district, particularly where the North Korean leadership is possibly hidden," to ashes (Park, 2016). ROK conventional attacks are unlikely to achieve such an outcome: During World War II, London was hit by over 500 V-2s but was not even close to being destroyed (Jones, 1992). Although a U.S. nuclear attack could achieve such an outcome, an attack on Pyongyang would generally be perceived in the United States as the targeting of civilians and contrary to U.S. nuclear weapon employment strategy.[8] Of course, this conclusion could be questioned depending on the threshold set for who in Pyongyang constitutes the regime that the Nuclear Posture Reviews threatens will not survive North Korean nuclear weapon use versus who in Pyongyang are civilians, as discussed in Chapter 1.

Some analysts have raised the concern that Kim might delegate nuclear launch authority to subordinate commanders. Indeed, his new laws in September 2022, as quoted in O'Carroll (2022), included a provision

> that in the event the "command and control system" of nuclear forces is "placed in danger" due to an attack from "hostile forces," then "a nuclear strike shall be launched automatically and immediately to destroy the hostile forces."

However, this statement might be primarily used for deterrence; it seems very unlikely that Kim's authoritarian government would not keep very tight control of its nuclear assets. China illustrated this kind of control for many years by keeping its nuclear weapons centrally stored despite the risk of a preemptive strike (Stokes, 2010).[9] Decapitation of the North Korean

---

[8] U.S. nuclear guidance

makes clear that all plans must also be consistent with the fundamental principles of the Law of Armed Conflict. Accordingly, plans will, for example, apply the principles of distinction and proportionality and seek to minimize collateral damage to civilian populations and civilian objects. The United States will not intentionally target civilian populations or civilian objects. (DoD, 2013, pp. 4–5)

[9] China appears to be dispersing its nuclear weapons, some to three ICBM silo fields and some to its ballistic missile submarines doing "at-sea deterrence patrols" (U.S. Office of the Secretary of Defense, 2022, pp. 64–65, 94).

regime has the potential of limiting the nuclear damage that North Korea could otherwise do.

Developing the Kill Web

The ROK Ministry of National Defense introduced the kill web operational concept in March 2023: "The Kill Web refers to a multilayered yet integrated apparatus that employs cyberoperations, electronic warfare tactics and other means to disrupt and negate the enemy's move to fire a missile even before its launch, according to a ministry official on condition of anonymity" (Song and Chae, 2023). It is expected that kill web can take great advantage of artificial intelligence by linking together these tools and the three-axis system, applying maximum military power on North Korea when required. The three-axis system has been focused on achieving outcomes with kinetic means, such as bombs and missile warheads. The kill web adds nonkinetic means that, at times, can be just as effective as kinetic means; it can also be used to maximize the effects of kinetic means by making sure that appropriate targets are identified, hit with precision, and truly eliminated. The kill web will provide advanced, enhanced, and integrated command and control for the ROK military forces and integration with U.S. forces as part of CFC. It will be part of Ministry of National Defense's Defense Innovation 4.0 (Song and Chae, 2023).

Developing Passive Defenses Against North Korean Nuclear Weapon Use

Passive defense is defined as "[m]easures taken to reduce the probability of and to minimize the effects of damage caused by hostile action without the intention of taking the initiative" (DoD, 2021, p. 165). Passive defense can consist of activities such as dispersal and evacuation, hardening (e.g., creating shelters), avoidance (e.g., marking contaminated areas to maneuver around them), decontamination, and other efforts to restore functions and services. Previous work by RAND and Asan described these options (Bennett et al., 2021, pp. 66–67). Because of Kim Jong-un's declared plans to use nuclear weapons to neutralize airfields (Kim and Smith, 2022), the ROK and United States could develop the ability to disperse and operate ROK and U.S. combat aircraft from their current dozen airfields to a much larger number of locations,[10] including highway landing strips.[11] Civilian protection could be enhanced by taking advantage of the nearly 19,000 shelters throughout the country, including 3,200 in Seoul, but treating these seriously by clearly marking them and stocking them with usable food, water, protective clothing, and radiation detection measures (Choi and Yang, 2017).[12]

Nuclear Warfighting

Now that Kim is consistently threatening to use nuclear weapons against the ROK and the United States, the ROK and United States must focus on planning for nuclear warfighting. If North Korea attacks the ROK or United States with nuclear weapons, that attack will be the beginning of a major war that the United States has declared would be the end of the Kim Family Regime. There appears to have been very little effort to characterize how

---

[10] We do not expect that North Korean nuclear weapons will have a high kill probability against airfields, because of limited missile and warhead reliability, limited accuracy and warhead yield, and ROK and U.S. missile defenses. Thus, North Korea might need to commit three to five (or more) nuclear weapons per ROK main airfield operating location and dispersal facility to neutralize them. With 12 combat airfields, that would be 36 to 60 (or more) nuclear weapons for just the main operating bases and two to three times that many if there were one or two dispersal airfields or landing strips per main base. That would be a very large number of nuclear weapons that North Korea might not be able to expend because it has other targets and requirements for second strikes and a nuclear strategic reserve force for seeking regime survival if the conflict goes badly for North Korea.

[11] In areas where adequate dispersal airfields do not currently exist, the ROK could examine its plans for building new roads. Where appropriate conditions exist, some new roads could simply be made wider than would otherwise be normally planned to allow for combat aircraft operations in a conflict; infrastructure could then be added along these highways to support such operations. Historically, the ROK had nearly a dozen highway landing strips that were prepared for this kind of purpose. But during the period in which the ROK and United States anticipated that reconciliation with North Korea might actually progress, most of these highway landing strips were abandoned. CFC has recently started testing the highway landing strip concept again (Senior CFC military officer, interview with Bruce Bennett, April 2023).

[12] Since the writing of this paragraph, the ROK has taken action to add the location of around 17,000 civil defense shelters to the web apps KakaoMap and Naver Map (Bremer, 2023).

such a conflict might unfold and differ from the focus of traditional ROK and U.S. planning, which has been initiated by a North Korean conventional invasion of the ROK. In this section, we discuss how such a process could proceed. Hopefully, the NCG would play a major role in such efforts.

In this area, the term *concept of operations* (CONOPS) is defined as a "verbal or graphic statement that clearly and concisely expresses what the commander intends to accomplish and how it will be done using available resources" (DoD, 2021, p. 45). CONOPS become key building blocks of any warfighting plan and conventional-nuclear integration when a country faces the North Korean nuclear weapon threat.

Iterative Concepts of Operation Development

During the Cold War, the United States and its NATO partners developed concepts for nuclear warfighting in Europe. Because the Soviets were perceived to have conventional-force superiority, the United States planned for early use of tactical nuclear weapons to stop Soviet breakthroughs along the front lines. Over time, the NATO CONOPS evolved to define in more detail how nuclear weapons would be used against a Soviet invasion. This work started from NATO intelligence on likely Soviet invasion concepts and proceeded to extensive CONOPS formulation and testing of alternative options.

A similar process could be pursued by the ROK and United States against a North Korean invasion. Starting from a common view of the North Korean threat as proposed earlier in this chapter, the ROK and United States could examine alternative approaches for countering that threat in different conditions. For example, as noted in Chapter 2, Kim has recently spoken several times about using tactical nuclear weapons carried by short-range ballistic missiles to neutralize ROK airfields. The ROK three-axis system is designed to counter such North Korean threats, but the timing of attack execution by each side matters considerably in terms of the damage that North Korea might do to the ROK airfields. The ROK and United States could therefore consider alternative outcomes of such North Korean nuclear attacks on ROK airfields and how to deal with them. That process would also inform ROK and U.S. efforts to enhance passive defenses, as described previously. The concept of a team of strategic advisers introduced in Chapter 3 could provide the personnel knowledgeable in these areas and in nuclear weapon operations to support CONOPS development.

CONOPS development is usually best done as an iterative process between concept formulation and testing of those concepts. The testing usually involves TTXs, analytic tools, and eventually some field exercises. For example, to sustain combat air operations, the Blue team doing CFC concept development might formulate an approach to having one dispersal airfield for each of the four or five primary ROK combat airfields. That concept could then be tested in a TTX with a Red team of experts in North Korean doctrine and operations. The Red team could formulate North Korean options for suppressing the ROK and U.S. combat airfields, including this dispersal airfield infrastructure. The TTX might demonstrate that having only four or five dispersal airfields would not be sufficient once the North Korean nuclear weapon force includes 80 to 100 nuclear weapons. The Blue team might then consider having ten to 12 dispersal airfields and seeing whether that size of infrastructure is sufficient for achieving the necessary level of CFC combat air operations survival. This iterative process would thus support CONOPS development and the efforts by the ROK and United States in determining how much defensive infrastructure is required in the ROK.

Establishing Combined Guidelines for Nuclear Weapon Employment

In 1962, McNamara offered to give U.S. allies a role in the "formulation of guidelines for the use of nuclear weapons." Such a role could be offered to the ROK and refined through the iterative CONOPS development process, which could be supported by the team of strategic advisers and likely be done by working groups of the NCG. These guidelines would be a fundamental element of ROK and U.S. planning for theater operations. The most-important guidelines related to nuclear weapons would be associated with the ROK and U.S. strategy for responding to a major North Korean invasion of the ROK supported by North Korean use of nuclear weapons.[13] Such

---

[13] Guidelines could also be established for various kinds of responses to North Korean limited nuclear attacks. For example, if North Korea launches a ballistic missile over the

guidelines do not need to define the specific targets for U.S. nuclear weapons but should talk about the strategic character of ROK and U.S. planning, including the conditions under which U.S. nuclear weapon use would be appropriate (e.g., a North Korean nuclear attack on ROK airfields) and the general kind of U.S. nuclear weapon use that could respond (e.g., striking the North Korean regime and nuclear weapon forces).

The ROK and United States could also develop a variety of other guidelines for U.S. nuclear weapon employment. These might include (1) the degree to which U.S. nuclear weapon use in retaliation against a North Korean nuclear weapon attack should be proportionate as opposed to overwhelming, (2) the distances from the ROK-China border within which U.S. nuclear weapons would normally not be used to avoid escalation with China, (3) nuclear employment standoff distances from Chinese forces (should they intervene) to also avoid escalation, (4) limitations on collateral damage expected from U.S. nuclear weapon use, (5) conditions under which nuclear weapon use might be considered against North Korean forces on ROK territory, (6) how much conventional versus nuclear firepower would be used against various kinds of targets, and (7) requirements for avoiding nuclear targeting of areas where ROK and U.S. special forces are operating in North Korea.

Such discussions would not be binding on the U.S. government but would hopefully allow the ROK and United States to have a common understanding of operating in a nuclear threat environment and conventional-nuclear force integration in response, especially once operational control is transferred to the ROK, with a ROK commander of CFC. Such an understanding would allow the ROK commander of CFC to direct the preparation of war plans for employing conventional forces and integration of those plans with potential U.S. nuclear weapon use.

Nuclear Weapon Employment Planning

The employment of U.S. nuclear weapons in North Korea would likely be a more incremental process than many might expect. For example, if North

---

East Sea and detonates a nuclear warhead on it that causes EMP damage to the ROK, what would be the scope and character of appropriate U.S. nuclear responses?

Korea uses nuclear weapons, the United States has promised that the regime will not survive. But it is fairly likely that the ROK and United States would not know where all of the key regime leaders are located at any given point in time. That is especially true once the fog of war descends on Korea. In addition, after a North Korean first nuclear attack, the ROK and United States will want to target the remaining North Korean nuclear weapons; ballistic missiles and other delivery means; and the nuclear command, control, and communications system as the other top-priority targets to prevent further nuclear damage to the ROK. And yet the ROK and United States are also unlikely to have perfect information on the location of many of these assets or targets, being forced to seek that information over time.

Table 4.1 provides a notional example of the potential first-priority targets for U.S. nuclear weapons in such a situation.[14] With regard to regime leaders, this example suggests that there might be regime leaders at two probable locations, another 12 locations that are suspected but with much less certainty, 13 possible locations, and a belief that there might be regime leaders at another eight locations that have not been located. Even if North Korea has fired an initial round of 20 or so nuclear weapons at the ROK, the United States is unlikely to fire several nuclear weapons at each of the 27 potential regime locations to destroy all of them, in part because such an attack would not be proportionate in size to the North Korean attack but also because some of these targets could be susceptible to conventional-weapon attacks.[15] Instead, the United States might fire several nuclear weapons at each of the

---

[14] In the immediate aftermath of a North Korean first nuclear strike on the ROK, it is likely that at least half of the North Korean nuclear weapons would not have been used in the North's first strike. As the number of North Korean nuclear weapons increases, the fraction of those withheld from a first strike could become much larger. The ROK and United States will likely place priority on nuclear attacks on the North Korean regime and its infrastructure that supports subsequent nuclear strikes against the ROK and other locations. Thus, we include in Table 4.1 the parts of the North's nuclear command, control, and communications system that are separate from the regime and the weapon facilities; the nuclear weapon storage facilities; the facilities potentially containing missiles that could be paired with nuclear weapons and have yet to be used; and the aircraft (both manned and drone) that could also be paired with nuclear weapons for delivery against the ROK.

[15] Even very reliable U.S. nuclear weapons and the missiles that carry them have a probability of 10 to 20 percent that they will not function as desired. To have a high probabil-

TABLE 4.1

Notional Example of First-Priority Targets for U.S. Nuclear Weapon Forces

	Number of Potential Targets of Each Type			
Location Type	Probable	Suspected	Possible	Not Identified
Regime leaders	2	12	13	8
Nuclear command, control, and communications[a]	1	5	0	0
Nuclear weapon storage	0	3	9	4
Missile facility[b]	11	15	19	22
Aircraft or drone facility[b]	6	7	21	10

[a] Separate from regime leaders and missile and aircraft or drone facilities.

[b] Facilities include bases and other storage and operating locations.

two probable and three or four of the suspected regime leader locations, along with the probable nuclear command, control, and communications facility; two or three of the suspected nuclear weapon storage facilities; and perhaps five or so of the probable missile facilities. If the United States targets two nuclear weapons at each of these locations, the United States would still be using 30 to 40 nuclear weapons and leaving dozens of potential targets for simultaneous conventional-weapon attacks. This kind of dynamic targeting using conventional-nuclear integration could then be used in subsequent attacks based on damage assessment of the initial U.S. attacks and developing intelligence. This process could be influenced by the nuclear weapon employment guidelines discussed previously.

Even this first nuclear weapon response may be only partially susceptible to detailed planning prior to the initiation of a crisis and the conflict. Once a crisis develops, the ROK and United States will apply much greater and intrusive intelligence collection than is normally used in peacetime, and that intelligence would adjust the numbers in Table 4.1. As the conflict continues, further intelligence will adjust the importance and likelihood of the various potential targets. For example, the ROK and United States might,

ity of destroying adversary targets, it is usually necessary to fire two to three warheads at each target from different ballistic missiles or other delivery means.

over time, assemble intelligence on the locations of the North's strategic reserve force of nuclear weapons and ballistic missiles and would then want to employ nuclear and conventional weapons, as appropriate, against those locations. The constantly changing warfare conditions and intelligence would require dynamic planning of U.S. nuclear and conventional-weapon attacks over time.

This process of refining target intelligence, developing packages of targets, and executing attacks that include U.S. nuclear forces is one key option that the United States could employ in training with the ROK.[16] Note that this process allows but does not require the United States to share current target information with the ROK. Instead, it could use a variant of Table 4.1 to develop the expertise and agility needed to prepare or modify nuclear and conventional attack packages once an actual conflict begins. Such exercises could also allow the U.S. government to share procedures with senior ROK leaders and secure agreement to the nuclear weapon employment guidelines discussed previously.

Obtaining ROK Government Approval of U.S. Nuclear Weapon Employment

As noted in Chapter 2, there appears to be no procedure for seeking ROK government approval, either in peacetime or during a conflict, for the use of U.S. nuclear weapons. Strictly speaking, the United States does not require foreign approval to use U.S. nuclear weapons. Nevertheless, there are many reasons for having such approval, including the ROK Constitution's declaration that North Korea is part of the ROK and potential postconflict ROK control of territories that have been subject to nuclear weapon attack.

If North Korea launches a major war against the ROK and uses nuclear weapons, there may be little time available to secure ROK leadership approval of a U.S. nuclear retaliation, many parts of which would likely

---

[16] The United States works with its NATO partners to train for just such nuclear and conventional attack operations in openly announced NATO field training exercises called Steadfast Noon ("NATO Begins Nuclear Exercises amid Russia War Tensions," 2022).

be urgent. As an example, using tactical nuclear weapons to stop a North Korean ground force breakthrough might require nuclear weapon employment to be ordered in an hour or less. There are five options for the United States to proceed relative to this issue:

1. The United States could decide to use nuclear weapons without ROK government consultation or approval.
2. The United States could inform the ROK when it plans to use nuclear weapons but not provide information on how or seek ROK approval.
3. The United States could work with the ROK to create the nuclear employment guidelines discussed previously, asking the ROK government to at least approve these guidelines.
4. The United States could involve ROK personnel in training to do dynamic nuclear weapon employment planning as outlined above and could seek ROK government reactions to the decisions on targeting made in the training exercises.
5. The United States could commit to seeking ROK government approval of actual nuclear weapon employment.

Within the context of the NCG, options 3 and 4 appear to be feasible and preferable to option 1. Option 5 would likely not be feasible because of the probable urgent nature of most U.S. nuclear attacks and the likely difficulty of communicating with the ROK government during wartime. There are many issues that would factor into a U.S. decision on these options.

Improve ROK and Japanese Defense Cooperation and Planning

In 2023, ROK President Yoon and Japanese Prime Minister Fumio Kishida held two summit meetings and made major efforts to reconcile the ROK and Japan, as urged by the United States ("Leaders from Japan and South Korea Vow Better Ties Following Summit," 2023). These meetings were followed by a U.S., ROK, and Japan trilateral summit, as noted previously. This reconciliation is required to coordinate defenses against North Korea, which is openly hostile toward both the ROK and Japan, and against China.

Thus, in one summit, the ROK and Japan agreed to link their radar systems to track North Korean missiles, likely enhancing their intelligence collection and increasing the probability of successful missile defense against a potential North Korean missile attack. By so doing, the ROK and Japan have increased deterrence against North Korean missile attacks. In addition, the earlier ROK-Japan summit saw the two leaders pledging to reinstate the "military intelligence-sharing pact between South Korea and Japan to better respond to North Korea's nuclear and missile threats" (Lee H., 2023b).

Nevertheless, this effort has been controversial in the ROK; the decades of Japanese occupation of Korea are a very difficult topic. Although increased ROK-Japan defense cooperation and planning is an option for the ROK, full cooperation could take some time.

CHAPTER 5

Nuclear Weapon Force Assurance Options

As noted in Chapter 1, public opinion surveys of the ROK population have shown for years that the majority of respondents in the ROK favor the ROK developing its own nuclear weapons:[1]

> Trends show growing support for indigenous nuclear program since 2019. There are several factors that may explain this trend: 1) the failure of nuclear negotiations with North Korea as of 2019; 2) the increased incidence of provocation and testing by North Korea; 3) the continued refinement and development of North Korean defense capability, including nuclear ones; 4) the growing concern about the longevity of U.S. security commitment to South Korea.[2] (Kim, Kang, and Ham, 2022, pp. 28–29)

All these factors have likely contributed to the decline in ROK nuclear assurance described in Chapter 2. North Korea is clearly building ICBMs and nuclear weapons to threaten the U.S. homeland. Once these North Korean threats are large enough, many question whether the U.S. nuclear umbrella will remain credible. North Korea appears short of posing such a threat today; Chapter 6 addresses when such a development might occur.

In this chapter, we describe some nuclear weapon force options that might provide the ROK with more tangible nuclear support today and in

---

[1] This chapter was prepared by Bruce W. Bennett and Uk Yang, with conceptual help from Myong-Hyun Go.

[2] Kim, Kang, and Ham (2022) shows poll results since 2010.

the coming few years. In particular, we consider in some detail ROK and U.S. options that would strengthen the nuclear weapon posture and commitments supporting the ROK. The continuing ROK focus on potentially acquiring ROK nuclear weapons or bringing U.S. tactical nuclear weapons back to the ROK should make it clear that nuclear weapon force options are probably the most important measures for strengthening ROK nuclear assurance. We also describe options for (1) providing greater presence of U.S. strategic systems in and around the peninsula; (2) explaining the adequacy of U.S. nuclear weapon forces for dealing with the combination of Russian, Chinese, and North Korean threats; and (3) explaining the safety and security of U.S. nuclear weapons. Note that these are descriptions and not analytic assessments of the relative utility of each option—ultimately the ROK and U.S. governments need to make such assessments with the sensitive information on nuclear forces available to them.

Potential Nuclear Weapon Commitment Options

In 1958, the United States deployed tactical nuclear weapons in the ROK to support deterrence of North Korean aggression. The number of those weapons reached a peak of around 1,000 weapons in 1967 and was then gradually reduced until the last were withdrawn at the order of President George H. W. Bush in 1991 (Kristensen, 2005b). Having nuclear weapons in the ROK gave a kind of visibility to the U.S. nuclear umbrella and appeared to assure that any major conflict on the peninsula could well involve U.S. nuclear weapon use—a strong deterrent of North Korean aggression and assurance of the ROK.

After 1991, ROK-U.S. deterrence of North Korean aggression was based on the conventional-force superiority of ROK and U.S. military forces when compared with the North Korean military forces. For years, senior U.S. military leaders have testified to Congress that they can deter and, if necessary, defeat North Korea (see Schwartz, 2002, pp. 6–7). It was not until North Korea began fielding nuclear weapons, and particularly after the first North Korean nuclear weapon test in 2006, that the U.S. nuclear umbrella once again became a major issue.[3] Since that time, the United States has chosen to depend primarily on its U.S.-based nuclear weapons for deterrence of North Korea and assurance of the ROK. Some in the ROK would like to have U.S. tactical nuclear weapons return to the ROK; others would like the ROK to produce its own nuclear weapons. Although the United States has many more nuclear weapons than North Korea will ever have, most U.S. nuclear weapons are dedicated for deterrence of or use against Russia and China and do not offset the North Korean nuclear weapon threat. Many in the ROK seek a clearer commitment of U.S. nuclear weapons to offset the North Korean nuclear weapon threat and achieve some degree of parity with that threat.

Constraints on Nuclear Weapon Commitments to the ROK

The ROK and United States have various constraints that need to be considered in formulating nuclear weapon commitment options. In terms of the United States providing nuclear weapons in or for the ROK, the first constraint is that the United States no longer has tens of thousands of nuclear weapons. Most of the U.S. nuclear weapon force was eliminated in the post–Cold War era, in part because it was not clear that nuclear weapons had much of a role in conflicts of that era and in part because of the advantages of nuclear arms control—reducing the likelihood of war, the potential cost of war, and the costs of preparation for war (Schelling, 1961). As of 2022, the United States had about 3,500 strategic nuclear weapons and another 200 tactical nuclear weapons; about 1,650 of the strategic weapons are avail-

---

[3] In the early 2000s, the United States had regularly promised the nuclear umbrella in the joint statement of the annual senior consultative meeting between the U.S. Secretary of Defense and the ROK Minister of National Defense. But in the 2005 senior consultative meeting, the ROK side asked that the wording *nuclear umbrella* be dropped from the joint statement; the United States refused. The 2006 senior consultative meeting was then held shortly after the first North Korean nuclear weapon test, and the ROK Minister of National Defense strove mightily to get Defense Secretary Donald Rumsfeld to promise an enhanced nuclear umbrella because of the nuclear weapon test (Kim, 2006).

able at any given time (Kristensen and Korda, 2022b).[4] That is a modest number for balancing the Russian, Chinese, and North Korean nuclear weapon forces and covering potential nuclear targets in those countries.[5] Although some U.S. strategic nuclear weapons might be committed to the ROK, the numbers would be limited. Moreover, the ongoing U.S. strategic nuclear weapon modernization program is designed to replace existing U.S. strategic nuclear weapon forces with somewhat fewer nuclear weapons, further constraining U.S. nuclear weapon availability.[6]

All the 200 or so U.S. tactical nuclear weapons are B61 nuclear gravity bombs, 100 of which are committed to NATO and based in Europe, while the other 100 bombs provide a global reserve force that is based in the United States (Kristensen and Korda, 2022b). Because of the limited size of this global reserve force, the United States is unlikely to draw from it and deploy dozens of these tactical nuclear bombs in the ROK in peacetime. In addition, there are only a few aircraft prepared for the delivery of these nuclear bombs. The fighter aircraft prepared for this role are referred to as *dual-capable aircraft* (DCA) because they can deliver either conventional or nuclear weapons.[7]

Nuclear weapon storage facilities are also a potential constraint. The last U.S. nuclear weapons based in the ROK were stored at Kunsan Air Base in 1991 (Kristensen and Norris, 2017); those nuclear weapon storage facili-

---

[4] The article notes that 400 ICBM warheads, 944 submarine-launched ballistic missile weapons, and 300 bomber weapons are available in peacetime.

[5] For example, Russia reportedly had some 2,600 strategic nuclear warheads and 1,900 tactical nuclear warheads (Kristensen and Korda, 2022a).

[6] For example, the current U.S. *Ohio*-class ballistic missile submarine force involves 14 ballistic missile submarines that are each allowed to carry 20 submarine-launched ballistic missiles, with four warheads allowed for each in the New START nuclear weapon treaty with Russia. The replacement *Columbia*-class ballistic missile submarine force will have 12 submarines that carry 16 missiles each, presumably with four warheads each. The number of missiles is thus reduced from 280 to 192 (O'Rourke, 2022, pp. 2–7). With Russia having abandoned New START, the United States could adjust the number of planned warheads for each missile to make up the difference if the United States chooses to, but that does not appear to be currently planned.

[7] These fighter aircraft are described as *dual-capable* because they can carry either conventional or nuclear weapons. Most U.S. fighter aircraft and all those owned by the ROK are not configured to carry nuclear weapons.

ties have not been used for nuclear weapon storage in more than 30 years. Those facilities would likely need to be refurbished if not replaced before moving any U.S. nuclear weapons to the ROK. At one point, nuclear bombs were also stored at Osan Air Base, but they were all removed in 1977; the Osan storage facilities have not been used for nuclear weapons in over 45 years (Kristensen and Norris, 2017). In addition, the ROK would presumably want to build such nuclear weapon storage facilities at ROK air bases to provide dispersal options for U.S. nuclear weapons and DCA and to protect any nuclear weapons the ROK might someday decide to produce.

Finally, the ROK does not have the uranium enrichment or plutonium reprocessing facilities necessary to produce the fissile material for nuclear weapons. Although the ROK has some uranium deposits, they have not been perceived as being commercially exploitable (Hansen, 1977). This condition poses a quandary for the ROK: It will want uranium for producing nuclear weapons, but if it abandons the Nuclear Non-Proliferation Treaty to build nuclear weapons, the Nuclear Suppliers Group is unlikely to provide the ROK with the needed uranium either for nuclear weapons or for its nuclear power industry. This quandary is discussed more in Chapter 6.

A Strategic, Coercive Approach for Enhanced Posture and Commitment

Many in the ROK think that deterrence of North Korea and assurance of the ROK would be strengthened by having nuclear weapons in the ROK, making nuclear weapons visible, and demonstrating that nuclear weapons are readily available for countering North Korean nuclear weapons use. Some would prefer that these be ROK government nuclear weapons, while others would be satisfied if some U.S. nuclear weapons were once again based in the ROK (Dalton, Friedhoff, and Kim, 2022, p. 2). In the short term, President Yoon rejected the option of ROK production of nuclear weapons in the Washington Declaration; we therefore postpone discussing this option until Chapter 6, where we look further into the future.

Note that the ROK and United States do not seek the commitment of enough nuclear weapons to the Korean theater to be clearly superior to the North Korean nuclear weapon force. In contrast, Robert McNamara sought to support NATO with a position of nuclear superiority relative to the Soviet nuclear weapon forces (1962, pp. 1–3). Rather, the ROK and United States would simply seek to avoid the appearance of North Korean nuclear dominance on the peninsula by maintaining a rough parity of nuclear forces to counter the North Korean nuclear weapon buildup.

The ROK and United States would clearly prefer to rein in the developing North Korean nuclear weapon threat to avoid a nuclear arms race on the peninsula, although they could prepare to counter the growth in North Korean nuclear weapons if the North is unresponsive to diplomacy. As noted in Chapter 3, the North Korean refusal to negotiate forces the ROK and United States to take coercive action against North Korea, seeking a verifiable CNM and nuclear weapon production freeze in the short term. Options that enhance the U.S. nuclear weapon commitments to ROK security seem ideal to help accomplish these objectives. Still, these actions should be taken incrementally to win ROK public and ROK and U.S. government understanding and to minimize the negative consequences already mentioned. There appears to be no discussion in the ROK of North Korea potentially posing a threat of 300 to 500 nuclear weapons, as noted in Chapter 2; it is only a future possibility that could push the ROK and United States into some of their more significant responses, which are likely not yet possible. If North Korea remains intransigent about developing a large nuclear weapon force, then this approach would help the ROK citizens, the Chinese, and even many North Koreans to know that the Kim Family Regime is responsible for the resulting instabilities. Hopefully, before that happens, the international community will once again agree to take serious action against North Korea to rein in its destabilizing behavior.

For the immediate future, we therefore propose an approach involving a family of four steps, taken over time,[8] each of which is a nuclear posture option to respond to the North Korean nuclear weapon buildup and to coerce a North Korean nuclear weapon and CNM production freeze. In practice, it might not be possible to get North Korea to implement such a freeze or at least slow its nuclear weapon buildup despite these coercive

---

[8] The ROK and United States could potentially add other incremental steps or options if the North's nuclear weapon developments are more limited, or they could combine some of these steps or options to move more rapidly if the North exponentially increases its pace of nuclear weapon production.

acts. But a North Korean threat of 300 to 500 nuclear weapons is an unacceptable future, giving the ROK and United States strong reasons for trying to prevent such an outcome. Thus, the ROK and United States could use this moderate approach to demonstrate to the ROK citizens, neighboring countries (such as China), and the international community that the ROK and United States are acting as clearly responsible parties to counter North Korea's efforts to exponentially increase its nuclear weapon threat. These four steps could be the following:

1. Modernize or build new U.S. nuclear weapon storage in the ROK at Kunsan Air Base and potentially at Osan Air Base.[9]
2. Dedicate all or part of the nuclear weapons on a U.S. ballistic missile submarine operating in the Pacific to targeting North Korea.
3. Modernize approximately 100 or U.S. tactical nuclear weapons—which the United States otherwise plans to dismantle—at ROK expense. These weapons would then be stored in the United States but would be committed to supporting the ROK. In a crisis or conflict, some of the warheads would be deployable to the nuclear weapon storage facilities in the ROK in a day.
4. Deploy a limited number of U.S. tactical nuclear weapons to the ROK to be stored in the prepared nuclear weapon storage facilities.

In introducing these steps, the ROK and United States could explain that they were remarkably patient and understanding while North Korea developed its defensive nuclear weapon posture and strategy. Now that North Korea has transitioned to focusing on an offensive nuclear weapon posture and strategy, the ROK and United States really have little choice but to balance the continuing North Korean nuclear weapon developments by achieving a degree of nuclear weapon parity that will assure the ROK people. Because North Korea already possesses a significant number of nuclear weapons, these steps could be pursued relatively rapidly in the absence of a reduction in North Korean nuclear weapon development. If the ROK and

---

[9] Because the U.S. tactical nuclear weapons are entirely B61 bombs at the time of writing, they would need to be stored at U.S. air bases in the ROK to be readily available for use against North Korea and simultaneously provide assurance to the ROK people.

U.S. threat assessment of North Korean nuclear weapons proposed in Chapter 4 confirms that North Korea already has sufficient CNM for more than 100 nuclear weapons, it might be necessary for the ROK and United States to advance from step to step as rapidly as every six months; the NCG could play a major role in recommending the implementation procedures and how rapidly this process ought to proceed.

The four steps are explored in further detail in the following sections.

Step 1: Nuclear Weapon Storage Facilities in the ROK

The ROK and United States could coerce North Korea by promising to modernize former nuclear weapon storage facilities in the ROK or build new ones unless the North verifiably freezes its CNM and nuclear weapon production. Because the remaining U.S. tactical nuclear weapons are all B61 nuclear bombs, the storage would need to be built at U.S. airfields in the ROK (Kunsan, Osan, or both), where they would be available to load on fighter aircraft and could be protected by U.S. security, as required by the Nuclear Non-Proliferation Treaty.

When the United States withdrew its tactical nuclear weapons from Korea, 100 nuclear weapons remained: 60 nuclear artillery shells (which are no longer available) and 40 B61 nuclear bombs (Kristensen and Norris, 2017, p. 352). The bombs were presumably stored in the same manner that B61 bombs have been stored for decades in Europe: Each of the bases with tactical nuclear weapons has "one or two dozen active vaults (weapons storage security system [WS3]) inside as many protective aircraft shelters" (Kristensen, 2022).[10] In the past, the WS3s were relatively secure against conventional-weapon attacks. As noted previously, these facilities likely need modernization if not replacement. By comparison, the facilities that support U.S. nuclear weapons in Europe has "been undergoing significant upgrades, including cables, command and control systems, weapons maintenance and custodial facilities, security perimeters, and runway and tarmac areas" (Kristensen, 2022). This modernization has been required to keep the European facilities in active use for storing the 100 U.S. tactical nuclear weapons that are deployed in Europe.

---

[10] Pictures of such storage can be seen in Kristensen (2022).

The ROK and United States could therefore consider two alternative possibilities for nuclear weapon storage in the ROK without specifically committing to placing nuclear weapons within these storage facilities. One approach would be to modernize the WS3 storage that was abandoned in 1991 at the Kunsan Air Base and in 1976 at the Osan Air Base. A thorough analysis of these facilities would need to be conducted and a decision made about whether modernization is economically feasible, including needed upgrades, as done in Europe, or whether new construction of WS3s is warranted. An alternative approach would be to build new storage facilities in Kunsan, Osan, or both that are designed to withstand North Korean nuclear weapon attacks. These new facilities would likely involve very hardened tunnels under these military air bases and very hardened access points. To isolate the effects of any North Korean nuclear weapon hit, the tunnels could have blast doors within the tunnels that would prevent damage to one part of the tunnels from spreading throughout the rest of the tunnels. Such a design would likely require the North to employ a large number of nuclear warheads against any military base with such nuclear weapon storage if the North wanted to destroy those weapons.[11]

This coercive threat—to build U.S. nuclear weapon storage in the ROK—could be made privately (i.e., to the North Korean delegation at the UN), although China could also be informed so that it might recognize the moderation of the ROK and U.S. approach.[12] When this ROK and U.S. effort eventually becomes known, it would demonstrate to the ROK people that the ROK and U.S. governments are concerned about the developing North Korean nuclear weapon threat and are striving to rein it in, a positive new direction. The ROK and United States could explain that they are not yet ready to put U.S. nuclear weapons in the ROK but that they intend to offset the North Korean nuclear weapon buildup. By providing the needed nuclear weapon storage, U.S. nuclear weapon deployment would be more feasible in the future. The ROK and United States would thus make it clear that,

---

[11] Presumably, other munitions and supplies could also be stored more safely in such tunnels, given the North Korean nuclear weapon threats.

[12] In contrast, Russia recently not only built nuclear weapon storage facilities in Belarus but also deployed nuclear weapons into those facilities. See Roth (2023). China has only expressed minimal criticism of the Russian actions (Kraterou and Evans, 2023).

although they are not anxious to put U.S. nuclear weapons in the ROK, they are preparing to do so if North Korea refuses to accept a production freeze. This approach would likely lead to less ROK political opposition than would deploying U.S. nuclear weapons to the ROK.

Step 2: U.S. Dedication of Strategic Nuclear Forces to Support the ROK

If step 1 fails to achieve a North Korean nuclear weapon and CNM production freeze, the ROK and United States could tell the world that they had tried to rein in North Korea, explaining step 1.[13] They could next coerce North Korea by promising to dedicate some number of nuclear weapons from the U.S. strategic arsenal for use against North Korea unless the North verifiably freezes its CNM and nuclear weapon production. For example, the United States could dedicate all or part of a ballistic missile submarine in the Pacific to targeting North Korea. There is a precedent for using this kind of approach to support U.S. allies. During the Cold War, the vulnerability of the nuclear weapons deployed in Europe led the United States to dedicate up to 400 nuclear weapons from what were perceived to be invulnerable Poseidon ballistic missile submarines to support NATO countries (Holcomb, 1976). Dedicating submarine-launched nuclear weapons to targeting North Korea would have limitations in achieving ROK nuclear assurance because these nuclear weapons would certainly not be as visible as ROK or U.S. nuclear weapons deployed in the ROK; however, they would not be vulnerable as those weapons would be. The current *Ohio*-class ballistic missile submarines carry 20 ballistic missiles with roughly four warheads per missile. Dedicating one such submarine for use against North Korea would imply a commitment of up to 80 nuclear weapons. That commitment could rotate as one submarine returns home and is replaced by another submarine.

---

[13] The ROK and United States could even explain that, since the step 1 offer, North Korea had produced another dozen (or whatever number) nuclear weapons, forcing the ROK and United States to take more serious actions. step 2 can therefore be characterized as North Korea's fault and not the fault of the ROK and United States. Note also that step 2 could be taken while the ROK and United States are modernizing or building nuclear weapon storage, because that storage is not required to take step 2.

As noted in the discussion of constraints, it is possible that, in light of the growing Chinese and Russian threats, the United States could find it difficult to dedicate an entire ballistic missile submarine to targeting North Korea. An alternative approach would be to dedicate part of a U.S. ballistic missile submarine to targeting North Korea. Another alternative would be to commit a U.S. nuclear weapon submarine to targeting both North Korea and China, which would be a stronger political statement supporting the ROK and a responsive action against the Chinese nuclear weapon buildup. Still, doing so could seriously offend China and increase the probability of some form of Chinese retaliation.

Step 3: Modernize U.S. Tactical nuclear weapons Held in the United States for Deployment to the ROK

If steps 1 and 2 fail to achieve a North Korean nuclear weapon and CNM production freeze, the United States could agree to let the ROK pay for modernizing 100 U.S. B61 nuclear bombs beyond those currently planned for modernization. The B61 bombs were originally built from the mid-1960s to the early 1990s for both strategic and tactical nuclear purposes, which, according to the Nuclear Weapon Archive (2023), left a large number of B61s still in service in 2020 and in need of modernization.[14] Facing budget constraints, the United States decided to modernize about 480 of these (to the B61-12 configuration) at a cost of about $10 billion (Kristensen and Korda, 2021a). Several hundred B61s, beyond the 480, could presumably still be modernized if funding is available and especially if the U.S. government were to think that the ROK government faced significant internal pressure to build its own nuclear weapons.

These bombs would still be U.S. nuclear weapons because the United States had already paid the entire original cost of producing the bombs being modernized. The ROK and United States could thus avoid any violation of the Nuclear Non-Proliferation Treaty. To reassure the ROK, the ROK and United States could sign an agreement to withhold these weap-

---

[14] The B61s are variable-yield bombs. Some are primarily tactical nuclear weapons, which have yields up to 50 kt. Others are primarily strategic and have yields up to 340 kt (Nuclear Weapon Archive, 2023).

ons for support of the ROK rather than allowing them to be used for other purposes. Because of the modernization cost for the planned 480 bombs, this step might cost the ROK $2 to $3 billion, far less than the potential ROK cost of building 100 of its own nuclear weapons, and also eliminates all of the potentially serious problems that the ROK would face in producing its own nuclear weapons (these problems are discussed further in Chapter 6). These bombs would be stored in the United States to protect them from North Korean attacks and from disruptive ROK demonstrations. The United States could rapidly deploy them to the ROK whenever a need arises because of the nuclear weapon storage created in step 1.

Step 4: Deploy a Limited Number of U.S. Tactical nuclear weapons in the ROK

If the previous steps fail to achieve a North Korean nuclear weapon and CNM production freeze, the ROK and United States could promise to deploy a limited number (perhaps eight to 12) of U.S. tactical nuclear bombs in the ROK, along with a few DCAs to deliver those weapons, if North Korea continues to refuse to freeze its nuclear weapon and CNM production. This action would take advantage of the preparation of required nuclear weapon storage in step 1.

Various experts in ROK national security think that deploying a few U.S. tactical nuclear weapons in the ROK would have a substantial ROK nuclear assurance effect by demonstrating a clear U.S. nuclear commitment to the ROK.[15] Doing so in step 4 and limiting the number of weapons deployed allows the previous three steps to condition both ROK audiences and the Chinese government that this action is taken because of North Korea's aggressive nuclear weapon buildup and intransigence on diplomacy, not because of ROK and U.S. aggressiveness.

Step 4 would have a further advantage. As the North Korean nuclear weapon inventory grows, at some point the North might conclude that it

---

[15] This number of nuclear weapons could eventually be taken from those that the ROK pays to modernize in step 3, although because of the time required to perform that modernization, these weapons may initially need to be taken from the U.S. tactical nuclear weapon reserve force in the United States.

can use nuclear weapons for demonstrations around the ROK or for limited nuclear attacks against the ROK. The United States worried about Soviet limited nuclear attacks in the late 1970s and in the 1980s. It developed "limited nuclear options" to deter small Soviet nuclear weapon attacks while doing extensive gaming to identify key vulnerabilities that the Soviets might seek to exploit with small nuclear weapon attacks and to determine how to deter such actions. Having a small number of nuclear weapons in the ROK would allow the ROK and United States to respond to any North Korean nuclear attack promptly (if the U.S. President decides to) and to particularly do so against any North Korean limited nuclear attack. The international community can expect that if North Korea targets the ROK with a limited nuclear attack, China and Russia will rapidly launch a psychological warfare campaign to convince world opinion that the ROK and United States need not respond with nuclear weapons. A few U.S. nuclear weapons in the ROK could allow the ROK and United States to execute a nuclear weapon response before significant Chinese or Russian interference and to do so with weapons that are clearly tactical nuclear weapons. This readiness could well help deter limited North Korean nuclear weapon attacks. Many ROK national security experts think that even a small number of U.S. nuclear weapons in the ROK will strengthen ROK nuclear assurance.

Timing the Steps

The ROK and United States would begin these steps from a position of apparent theater nuclear inferiority, with no U.S. nuclear weapons committed to supporting ROK security.[16] Therefore, at least the first two steps ought to be taken no more than a year or two apart from each other, but would be best taken separated by about six months. Of course, the United States would be highly unlikely to complete either modernization of its nuclear weapon

---

[16] Many will perceive that the United States has a very large number of nuclear weapon forces that are clearly offsetting the nuclear weapon forces of North Korea. But most of the U.S. nuclear weapon forces are committed to deterring Russian and Chinese use of nuclear weapons, with the Chinese nuclear weapon force growing rapidly. Thus, from a ROK perspective, U.S. strategic ambiguity could well be interpreted as the United States talking tough but lacking the resources to adequately counter the North Korean nuclear weapon threat.

storage in the ROK or new construction of such storage within a six-month period. It would thus be the announcements of these steps that would be separated by six months rather than the completion of each step leading to the initiation of the next step. That would be particularly true when considering steps 3 and 4: Completion of the modernization of 100 nuclear weapons as part of step 3 could take several years. Instead, if North Korea has not frozen its nuclear program around six months after step 3 is announced, it would be appropriate to announce step 4. These four steps would hopefully create more of an appearance of balance in the nuclear weapons available to each side on the Korean Peninsula, strengthening ROK nuclear assurance; given the North's initial nuclear inventory, full numerical parity might be delayed until the actions proposed in Chapter 6 are taken.

Adjusting the Family of Nuclear Weapon Commitment Options

These four steps or options have been chosen to provide appropriate, relatively simple, escalating responses to the North Korean nuclear weapon buildup. These options could help the ROK people understand over time how serious the North Korean growth in nuclear weapons is becoming. These steps also seek to minimize negative responses within the ROK and from China and North Korea. However, they are not the only options. Some alternatives could add steps: For example, between steps 1 and 2, the ROK could threaten North Korea that, unless it freezes its nuclear weapon production program, the ROK will build nuclear weapons storage facilities at its military air bases to provide dispersal options for U.S. nuclear weapons and DCA in crises and conflict. As an alternative or addition to step 2, the United States could threaten to rearm with nuclear weapons one or more of its aircraft carriers operating in the western Pacific, making it able to provide nuclear weapon responses against North Korean nuclear weapon attacks. And the ROK and United States could agree to build and jointly crew several submarines that carry ballistic missiles with nuclear warheads, such as the Multilateral Force that the United States tried to set up in the 1960s with its NATO allies. In addition, step 3 could be modified to involve modernizing only a few dozen nuclear weapons (instead of 100) as a starting point, with options to expand the number should North Korea remain unresponsive.

If the ROK and United States are not able to freeze the North Korean nuclear weapon buildup in the next few years, a series of other options could also be considered. These options are discussed in Chapter 6.

Handling Negative Reactions

The downsides of these steps are the cost of implementing them and any potential backlash from within the ROK and from North Korea and China. The cost would depend on the options chosen. For example, given the status of the existing WS3 facilities, would step 1 involve mainly WS3 modern-ization versus new construction of nuclear weapon storage? How protected would that new storage be? Some ROK political demonstrations would likely be expected in response to either alternative but not nearly as much as deploying a significant number of tactical nuclear weapons in the ROK.

These steps will not be particularly appealing to North Korea or China, both of which apparently want to achieve some degree of subjugation of the ROK. Such an outcome would be unacceptable to both the ROK and United States. The inadequacy of ROK and U.S. offsetting of actions in recent years appears to have been a major source of the declining nuclear assurance among the ROK population. ROK and U.S. action could hopefully stop this decline and rebuild ROK trust and assurance. These offsets would also hope to sustain deterrence of North Korea.

North Korea would be expected to make major responses with both information and provocations, forcing the ROK and United States to plan from the beginning how they would respond to such actions and warning the North about potential ROK and U.S. responses. China will also be unhappy about these developments, but the ROK and United States could explain to China that they are taking a very moderate set of actions in response to the ongoing North Korean escalation of its nuclear weapon threat, which China has been allowing and even though it is also a threat to China. At each stage, the ROK and United States wish to avoid escalation, but doing so will only be possible if North Korea ceases its nuclear weapon and CNM production. It is therefore hoped that China would bring North Korea back to negotiations, if China is able to, and to induce North Korea to freeze its nuclear weapon and CNM production.

Some Observations on the Commitment Steps

The steps outlined here are intended to show growing ROK and U.S. commitment and resolve against the North Korean nuclear weapon buildup to reassure the ROK population. Ideally, they will be sufficient to induce at least a partial North Korean nuclear weapon and CNM production freeze, which would hopefully be very reassuring to the ROK people. But if North Korea refuses to rein in its nuclear weapon and CNM production effort, as we expect, these steps are intended to achieve a degree of parity with the growing North Korean nuclear weapon threat. There are costs to these steps both monetarily and in terms of potential political problems in the ROK and with North Korea and China. But if North Korea's nuclear buildup continues, the ROK will increasingly feel subject to coercion and potential attack by North Korea.

There is a further potential risk to taking this approach. Although President Yoon is expected to support steps like these, a future ROK president might be unwilling to do so. Indeed, a future ROK president could renounce some or all of the steps outlined here, returning the ROK to a position of serious vulnerability to the North Korean nuclear weapon threat, which, by that stage, would be larger. The likelihood of such an outcome could be reduced by explaining to the ROK people the need for this kind of action to develop national ROK consensus on the moderation, yet potential effectiveness, of this approach. That consensus would be extremely important because it can certainly be expected that North Korea will make every effort to undermine these steps.

Deploying U.S. Strategic Weapon Systems to the Peninsula

One measure President Yoon had reportedly considered before the Washington Declaration was to have at least one U.S. strategic weapon system deployed constantly in or near the ROK in response to growing North Korean threats:

> South Korea has asked the United States to have strategic assets, such as nuclear aircraft carriers or nuclear submarines, deployed to waters around the Korean Peninsula on a rotational basis around the clock in the event of a nuclear test by the North. . . . The U.S. strategic assets that are being talked about as candidates for rotational deployment are the U.S.S Ronald Reagan aircraft carrier, B-1, B-2 and B-52 strategic bombers and nuclear-powered submarines. (Lee H., 2022)

Only some of these systems can currently carry nuclear weapons, including ballistic missile submarines, but they all still have a strategic character. In fact, the ROK apparently prefers such deployments to the deployment of U.S. nuclear weapons to the ROK.[17]

The advantages of these deployments include strengthening the ROK-U.S. alliance by familiarizing ROK forces with these strategic systems and demonstrating a U.S. willingness to commit such systems in support of the ROK. These deployments are also coming in response to North Korea's extensive missile tests in 2022, although it would have been better to threaten to make these deployments first to deter more North Korean missile tests and then make more deployments if North Korea continued its tests.[18]

The disadvantages of these deployments begin with the cost to the United States in both monetary terms and force usage. That is, regularly operating forces in the ROK requires that appropriate maintenance and support capabilities also exist in the ROK, where support for U.S. strategic systems is minimal because none are based in the ROK. Having these forces regularly

---

[17] For the ROK, "It is 'most desirable' to deter the North using 'U.S. strategic assets currently available on the Korean Peninsula,' rather than deploying U.S. tactical nuclear weapons, Vice Minister of National Defense Shin Beom Chul told SBS Radio on Thursday" (Choi, 2022c).

[18] This is an example of the problem with threatening North Korea using strategic ambiguity. Had the United States used strategic clarity and specifically threatened this action, North Korea might have chosen not to launch some of its missile tests. If it continued launching missiles, everyone in the region and around the world would know that these deployments are not an aggressive act by the United States but a defensive act against North Korean provocations.

deployed to the ROK would require an assessment of whether the nuclear forces would need to be replaced in their current locations. If so, the United States could acquire other forces to replace the systems that are regularly deployed to the ROK.[19]

The costs also include handling the potential of North Korean escalation in response to these deployments. The United States has traditionally sought to avoid any escalation with North Korea that could lead to some form of conflict through an escalation spiral, a particular danger when Kim is acting with serious paranoia in response to U.S. training in the ROK and other deployments.

Explaining U.S. Nuclear Weapon Availability and Safety

The number of U.S. nuclear weapons peaked at about 31,000 in 1967 but by 2022 had fallen to about 3,700 active (strategic and tactical) nuclear weapons (Kristensen and Norris, 2013). The United States could analytically demonstrate to the ROK that this number is sufficient to deal with the nuclear weapon threats from Russia, China, and North Korea. Such an explanation could contribute significantly to ROK nuclear assurance, especially if the United States pursues further nuclear weapon arms control. But without such an explanation, at least some national security experts in the ROK are likely to question the sufficiency of U.S. nuclear weapons—questioning that would undermine ROK nuclear assurance.

In addition, international experts have had some reason to question the safety and security of U.S. nuclear weapons. In 2007, a U.S. nuclear bomber was accidentally loaded with six real nuclear cruise missiles instead of surrogate devices and flown from North Dakota to Louisiana. In 2006, four electrical fuses for Minuteman nuclear warheads were accidentally flown to Taiwan and stored there (Shanker, 2008). The former caused both the U.S. Air Force Secretary and the Chief of Staff to be fired; the latter led to the disciplining of 15 senior U.S. Air Forces officers (Losey, 2019). The United

---

[19] Although the ROK has strongly encouraged these deployments, it has not publicly offered to cover any of these costs.

States could explain that the lack of such incidents since these demonstrate that U.S. nuclear weapons are safe and secure. The United States could also explain to the ROK government the security improvements that have been made since those events, if this has not already been done. This explanation could be done in support of the 2023 Washington Declaration.

CHAPTER 6

ROK Nuclear Assurance in Changing Conditions

In Chapters 3 through 5, we described a variety of options that the United States and the ROK could implement to strengthen ROK nuclear assurance in the short term.[1] We assume that some of these could be implemented while others might not be. As the North Korean nuclear weapon threat grows and other conditions change, the importance of the options not implemented will likely change and cause the ROK and the United States to revisit those options. Although we certainly hope that the options in Chapters 3 to 5 push North Korea into a nuclear weapon and CNM production freeze, we do not expect such an outcome: Kim Jong-un has built too much of his power base on his nuclear weapons. It is therefore reasonably probable that in five to 20 years North Korea will have fielded a large force of 200 to 300 or more nuclear weapons.[2] In that period, China is also expected to field a nuclear weapon force that will begin to rival those of the United States and Russia, as discussed in Chapter 2.

In this chapter, we take a longer-term perspective and describe options for strengthening ROK nuclear assurance as the North Korean and Chinese nuclear weapon threats increase significantly. We begin by summarizing the

---

[1] This chapter was prepared by Bruce W. Bennett and Kang Choi.

[2] It is noted in Chapter 2 that Kim Jong-un appears to be seeking an inventory of 300 to 500 nuclear weapons. If he can exponentially increase his nuclear weapon production, a North Korean force of 300 nuclear weapons might exist in approximately five to ten years. This increase in production might be especially possible with Russian assistance, such as the centrifuges Russia provided two decades ago (Heinonen, 2011). This force is much larger than what North Korea needs for deterrence or defensive purposes and could likely do existential damage to the ROK and Japan.

ROK and U.S. options that will hopefully be in place before North Korea has built a large nuclear weapon force of 200 to 300, or more, nuclear weapons. We then address the importance of the strategic clarity of the U.S. nuclear umbrella, paying particular attention to a sequence of measures from Chapters 3 through 5 that, if not yet implemented, could be used, largely mirroring the U.S. efforts planned with NATO in the 1960s as a point of reference. We then revisit the options for supporting the ROK with nuclear weapon forces, recognizing that the ROK government might feel increasing pressure to have available nuclear weapons beyond those offered as options in Chapter 5. Unfortunately, there are few ROK and U.S. nuclear weapon commitment options at that point, a difficult quandary with which the ROK and United States need to come to terms. But North Korea also needs to understand the potential impacts of its continued production of nuclear weapons and CNM.

Strengthening ROK Nuclear Assurance Before North Korea Creates a Large Nuclear Weapon Force

Some of the options described in Chapters 3 to 5 appear more likely to strengthen ROK nuclear assurance, especially if North Korea continues to refuse to rein in its nuclear weapon development program. These options are the following, listed from the easiest options to implement to the more effective, but more difficult to implement options:

1. Implement a dynamic and capable NCG, which would be assisted by a team of strategic advisers, to bring strategic clarity to the U.S. nuclear umbrella extended to the ROK.[3]

---

[3] President Yoon has been very clear that he thinks that strategic clarity is needed to strengthen ROK nuclear assurance. In early 2023, he argued that the "nuclear weapons belong to the U.S., but the planning, information sharing, exercises and training should be carried out jointly by South Korea and the U.S." (Lee, 2023c).

2. Educate ROK and U.S. national security personnel on the implications of the North Korean nuclear weapon threat and what can be done about it.

3. Develop more ROK public awareness of the North Korean nuclear weapon threat and the actions that are being taken to counter it.

4. Shift the focus of conflict planning in CFC to conventional-nuclear force integration, including regular TTXs that assist in strategy formulation.

5. Establish ROK and U.S. nuclear weapon employment guidelines, exploiting the regular TTXs, and seek ROK and U.S. National Command Authority approval of them.

6. Use a full variety of coercive measures to induce a North Korean nuclear weapon and CNM production freeze.

7. Use the four-step approach outlined in Chapter 5 to create a baseline U.S. nuclear weapon commitment to ROK security.

    a. This approach could commit up to 180 nuclear weapons to ROK security, with perhaps eight to 12 B61 nuclear bombs deployed in the ROK.

    b. As noted in Chapter 5, the incremental nature of this approach is intended to moderate responses to the ROK and U.S. actions both inside the ROK and by China.

Example: Using Tabletop Exercises to Help Strengthen ROK Nuclear Assurance

North Korean nuclear weapon–related coercion is already one of the biggest factors undermining ROK nuclear assurance. When North Korea has 300 nuclear weapons, the North will likely be regularly pressing the ROK that the U.S. nuclear umbrella is no longer meaningful; at that point, North Korea would claim to have sufficient nuclear weapons to destroy U.S. cities should the United States exercise the nuclear umbrella and retaliate against North Korean nuclear weapon use on the ROK. Kim apparently wants the ROK to believe that the United States would not be willing to accept the risk of nuclear weapon attacks on the United States and would therefore abandon the ROK. As argued in Chapter 2, North Korea hopes to use this kind of coercion to decouple the ROK-U.S. alliance.

It will therefore be important that the United States reiterates its commitments to the nuclear umbrella and explains why the ROK population should not believe the North Korean argument. One of the best ways to accomplish this latter task may be to regularly (perhaps monthly) have the NCG working groups carry out a TTX of North Korean nuclear weapon use (as promised in the Washington Declaration) that tests such cases. Then, to assist the ROK public's nuclear assurance, at least some summaries of the TTXs could be openly published, especially those that contradict the apparent North Korean argument.

For example, a future TTX could test Kim's decoupling hypothesis. Although teams could play such a situation differently, consider a 2030 case in which North Korea invades the ROK and immediately uses 50 nuclear weapons against ROK airfields, ports, and military command and control, the targets Kim that has explicitly threatened. Simultaneously, he threatens the United States that if any U.S. nuclear weapons are used to retaliate against his nuclear attacks on the ROK, cities in the United States will be attacked by North Korean ICBMs with nuclear weapons. A TTX could use standard intelligence assessments to provide a perspective for potential outcomes, providing a reference case to help TTX participants establish perceptions of Kim's likely capabilities. The TTX might show that, despite North Korean attempts to use 50 nuclear weapons against the ROK, 15 of the missiles and nuclear warheads would probably fail to function properly,[4] 30 would likely be shot down by ROK and U.S. missile defense, and only five would likely arrive at their targets and cause damage. Although a substantial amount of damage would be done to those five targets, by 2030 the ROK and United States could have dispersed combat aircraft from their normal

---

[4] The North Korean ballistic missile testing program apparently seeks to make the North Korean ballistic missiles appear to be highly reliable and to almost always have successful flights. Nevertheless, it is not known how often North Korea attempts to launch a ballistic missile and nothing happens. It is also unknown how often the North Korean missiles shot out into the oceans fly their intended trajectory and deliver a payload anywhere near the intended target. Moreover, we can expect that the missiles that North Korea tests have been thoroughly inspected and prepared for reliable launches; the missiles actually launched in an operational situation are less likely to be so reliable. Indeed, some kind of failure of perhaps 30 percent or more of North Korea's operationally launched ballistic missiles seems fairly likely.

military airfields and dispersed other resources associated with major ports and military command and control, limiting that damage.

In this TTX, assume that the U.S. team remains true to its nuclear umbrella and launches a proportionate nuclear weapon counterleadership and countermilitary attack against North Korea, eliminating Kim and much of his senior leadership and destroying most of the residual North Korean nuclear weapons and ballistic missiles. Nevertheless, in the TTX a North Korean leadership successor can launch five ICBMs with nuclear weapons at U.S. cities. One of those fails, three are shot down by U.S. missile defense, and only one arrives at a U.S. city. That disaster leads to a major follow-on U.S. retaliation against North Korea, destroying North Korean political and military command-and-control facilities, as well as most of the North Korean residual nuclear weapons and associated ballistic missiles and launchers. The United States would not be pleased with such an outcome, nor would anyone in North Korea once they heard a summary of such a TTX. Meanwhile, many in the ROK would likely feel considerable nuclear reassurance in such a case because they would perceive that the observed destruction of North Korea in the TTX would deter Kim from ever trying such an attack in the first place.

The results of such TTXs would hopefully build ROK nuclear assurance. The TTXs would also likely show that, in cases in which North Korea used nuclear weapons against the ROK, the United States would respond against North Korea using nuclear weapons. Thus, although a U.S. President might be reluctant to make such a statement, the results of the TTXs could demonstrate U.S. commitment to the ROK.

Nuclear Weapon Force Commitments to the ROK Against a Large North Korean Nuclear Weapon Force

Discussions with ROK personnel suggest that, for them to feel nuclear assurance, they want the appearance of parity between North Korean nuclear weapons and U.S. nuclear weapons that are specifically committed to ROK security.[5] Because the current specific U.S. nuclear weapon commitment to the ROK is zero, many in the ROK think that North Korea is militarily superior to the ROK when nuclear weapons are included in the military balance (Lee et al., 2023, pp. 56–58), which many U.S. analysts find incredible given the U.S. nuclear umbrella. This situation reflects the lack of strategic clarity in the nuclear umbrella. Although nuclear parity is admittedly a requirement to support the ROK psychologically, in a similar manner the nuclear weapon balance between United States and the Soviet Union was a major issue for decades (see, for example, Bennett, 1980a), which included U.S. concerns in the late 1950s that a missile gap was developing (Thielmann, 2011) and likely prompted Robert McNamara's statement to NATO allies in 1962 that the United States had and would maintain nuclear weapon superiority over the Soviet Union (McNamara, 1962, pp. 3, 5, 6).

If North Korea fields a large force of 200 to 300 or more nuclear weapons, the establishment of a level of parity of U.S. versus North Korean nuclear weapons will almost certainly be a major factor in ROK nuclear assurance. The four steps in Chapter 5 might result in a commitment of up to 180 or so U.S. nuclear weapons supporting the ROK, but more nuclear weapons could eventually be required to maintain the appearance of parity. Reaching even 180 committed nuclear weapons would require U.S. dedication of an entire ballistic missile submarine (step 2 in Chapter 5) and ROK financing of 100 B61 modernizations (step 3 in Chapter 5); both the ROK and United States could decide to commit a smaller number in each case. Indeed, with the growing Chinese nuclear weapon threat, the United States might not be prepared to dedicate an entire ballistic missile submarine to ROK security, let alone more. Thus, even reaching 180 nuclear weapons could require new options.

In practice, there appear to be only the following three options available if North Korea builds a large nuclear weapon force:

- Drop the concept of maintaining a degree of parity with the North Korean nuclear weapon forces.

---

[5] This statement is based on many discussions of Bruce Bennett with ROK national security personnel since roughly 2016 (ROK security officials, interviews with Bruce Bennett, 2016–2023).

- Create some form of combined ROK-U.S. funding of new nuclear weapons committed to the ROK beyond the 100 weapons recommended in step 3 of Chapter 5.
- Allow the ROK to produce its own nuclear weapons.

These are all disagreeable choices that are accompanied by considerable risks. They clearly demonstrate that reining in the North Korean nuclear weapon production to around 200 to 300 nuclear weapons or fewer, which might avoid these alternatives, is highly desirable. But that may not be possible, and therefore the ROK and United States could consider these alternatives as options that they might face in the future.

Drop the Concept of Maintaining Parity with the North Korean Nuclear Weapons

Despite all the public opinion polls conducted in the ROK that ask about support for the ROK's development of its own nuclear weapons, it is unknown exactly how the various potential factors affect ROK nuclear assurance. Nevertheless, there appears to be strong ROK interest in maintaining some degree of parity with the North Korean nuclear weapon forces. Indeed, in the 1960s, the United States told its NATO allies that it would maintain nuclear superiority over the Soviet Union to avoid their nuclear proliferation (McNamara, 1962, pp. 1 and 3). But, as described in Chapter 5, the large number of U.S. strategic nuclear weapons currently plays little role in the assessment of parity with North Korea because it is known in the ROK that most those weapons are committed against Russia and China and not available for use against North Korea.

The four-step approach presented in Chapter 5 seeks to maintain a degree of parity between the North Korean nuclear weapon forces and nuclear weapons that the United States commits to supporting ROK security. However, as the size of the North Korean nuclear weapon threat approaches 300 weapons, the United States might decide that it cannot maintain that parity. We do not know how such a U.S. decision would affect ROK nuclear assurance, although we suspect it would have a very negative impact. That decision might significantly increase ROK support for an independent nuclear weapon force and become the deciding factor in the ROK government making such a decision. The United States government might therefore need to recognize that the option of abandoning parity poses significant risks to the U.S. objective of preventing ROK nuclear proliferation.

Fund a Further Expansion of U.S. Nuclear Weapon Forces

The second option involves combined ROK and U.S. payments for modernizing or building U.S. tactical nuclear weapons beyond the 100 weapons proposed in Chapter 5. This option would add U.S. nuclear weapons to cover requirements in the ROK without having to take U.S. nuclear weapons away from targets in Russia, China, or other countries. The United States is not prepared to increase the number of its strategic nuclear weapons because of the New START treaty with Russia and the cost of doing so. Although Russia has suspended its implementation of this treaty, the United States does not want to appear to be violating this treaty and might continue that position even after the treaty ends in 2026 (Landay and Mohammed, 2023). Thus, any expansion of U.S. nuclear weapons to offset the growth in North Korean nuclear weapons would likely need to be done with U.S. tactical nuclear weapons, which are not limited by New START.

There are a few tactical nuclear weapon possibilities that could be used to sustain parity if North Korea builds 300 or more nuclear weapons. If the United States acts promptly to delay any further dismantlement of B61 nuclear bombs, it might be able to have available several hundred of these nuclear weapons for modernization in support of ROK security. Beyond the first 100 nuclear weapons discussed as step 3 in Chapter 5, the ROK and United States might want to work out a procedure for sharing the cost of modernization. Like with the first 100 weapons, these would still be U.S. nuclear weapons that would be best stored in the United States to protect them and avoid political confrontation in the ROK. Alternatively, the U.S. military services are developing theater ballistic missiles that are projected to become available as early as 2024 or 2025 (see, for example, Feickert, 2022, and Bosbotinis, 2022). Some of these missiles could be adapted to deliver tactical nuclear weapons and placed in the ROK or on U.S. Navy platforms surrounding the peninsula to provide this support. Indeed, the United States had planned to build a nuclear submarine-launched cruise missile until it was canceled by the U.S. 2022 Nuclear Posture Review (DoD, 2022b). That program could potentially be reinstated.

There are several principal advantages of using enhanced production of U.S. tactical nuclear weapons to sustain parity with the North Korean nuclear weapon program. The key advantage would be that this approach might be able to avert ROK production of nuclear weapons that could undermine the international Nuclear Non-Proliferation Treaty and potentially lead to nuclear weapon production by countries that do not yet have nuclear weapons. In addition, sustaining nuclear parity with North Korea would likely provide nuclear assurance for the ROK and deterrence of North Korean nuclear weapon attacks and possibly North Korean nuclear weapon coercion.[6] This parity would also give North Korea incentives to consider a freeze of its nuclear weapon production, which would not be gaining it any significant advantage in this case. Storing most of these weapons in the United States would also prevent North Korea from posing a serious counterforce threat against them, could limit ROK political action by those opposed to nuclear weapons, and could reduce the Chinese response to this expansion. Finally, this approach would provide incentives for CFC to engage ROK personnel with U.S. nuclear planners, thereby strengthening the ROK-U.S. alliance.

Nevertheless, this approach also has some downsides. Of particular concern is that, as the number of nuclear weapons would grow in North Korea and for the ROK and United States, there is a potential for instability on the peninsula. Both sides might consider a preemptive counterforce attack. Still, this might cause less instability than allowing North Korea to deploy a superior nuclear force against the ROK. In addition, many in the United States will not be anxious to see a growth in the number of U.S. nuclear weapons, even if that growth is only in tactical nuclear weapons. The ROK and United States could also work out how to pay for this effort cooperatively; that cost would likely force the ROK and United States to forgo some

---

[6] As noted previously, we freely admit that comparing the numbers of committed nuclear weapons on the two sides is a very limited view of the nuclear balance. However, there is not a general understanding of nuclear balance assessments, and therefore attention often focuses on the numbers. We expect that this understanding might also be true for Kim.

conventional-force weapon systems. Neither the ROK nor the U.S. military forces are likely to be anxious to have to provide the military personnel who could employ these weapons in a conflict.

Some in the ROK also want to have ROK nuclear weapon sharing that would be analogous to the nuclear weapon sharing in NATO (which involves nuclear weapon delivery by host-nation pilots once keys are employed by both U.S. and allied officials).[7] Because many in the United States are dissatisfied with NATO nuclear weapon sharing,[8] it is unlikely that the United States will want to make such an arrangement in the ROK. Nuclear weapon sharing with the ROK could first involve the ROK paying to modernize some U.S. nuclear bombs for deployment to the ROK and acquiring DCA designed to deliver those nuclear bombs. Using the NATO example, nuclear sharing would then mean building the required nuclear weapon storage at a ROK air base, putting some of these bombs at the base with a U.S. security force adequate to maintain control of and protect the weapons (as required by the Nuclear Non-Proliferation Treaty), and stationing nuclear control officers who are prepared to release the weapons to the ROK and providing them with secure nuclear cleared communications to authorize this action. Doing so at a ROK air base would require considerable U.S. expense and increase the vulnerability of U.S. nuclear weapons to determined terrorists or other rogue groups. The United States would also worry that once it releases the nuclear weapons, it would have no direct control over where the weapons would be delivered. Moreover, a future ROK president could abort the entire program, making the U.S. investment of funds and effort a waste. What would the ROK gain other than political appearances? If some form of sharing would really be helpful, why not consider adding a few ROK pilots to a future U.S. squadron prepared to deliver nuclear bombs if the bombs are placed in the ROK? Alternatively, the United States could simply

---

[7] There is considerable confusion in the ROK about the meaning of nuclear sharing. The use of this concept in NATO has made it of interest to some in the ROK. But the journal article by Kort et al. (2019) recommending nuclear sharing in the ROK increased the visibility of the subject. It is now given a variety of meanings beyond the term applied in NATO. See Ahn (2022).

[8] U.S. government personnel, interviews with Bruce Bennett, 2012–2023.

agree with ROK President Yoon that the Washington Declaration is already "'more effective' than NATO's analog for nuclear sharing" (Reddy, 2023b).

The ROK's Production of Its Own Nuclear Weapons

The third option is for the ROK to produce its own nuclear weapons, which is the apparent preference of the ROK people, consistent with the findings of ROK public opinion polls (see, for example, Kim, Kang, and Ham, 2022). This option would provide recognition that the ROK is a major power, "increasing South Korea's prestige in the international community" (Dalton, Friedhoff, and Kim, 2022, p. 2).[9] The ROK might especially expect such recognition if it builds hundreds of nuclear weapons to maintain parity with the number of North Korean nuclear weapons projected in this report. The option would also give the ROK discretion in its use of nuclear weapons against North Korea and allow the ROK to pose threats against the North that are stronger than those threats that United States has been willing to pose and therefore could increase both deterrence of North Korean nuclear weapon use and ROK nuclear assurance.

However, it seems likely that many ROK government leaders and the ROK public have not appreciated how serious the potential risks and downsides are of this option (Brewer and Dalton, 2023).[10] First, North Korea would strongly object and likely cause serious crises, including committing major provocations, trying to prevent having nuclear weapons in the ROK. Second, ROK progressives would likely object, as would ROK citizens living near whichever military bases would be chosen for nuclear weapon storage, knowing that their communities would become high-priority nuclear

---

[9] This poll reports that the main reasons respondents gave regarding a ROK nuclear weapon program are (1) defending the ROK from threats other than North Korea (39 percent), (2) increasing ROK international prestige (26 percent), (3) countering the North Korean threat (23 percent), and (4) fearing that the United States will not defend the ROK if it is attacked (10 percent). But this poll was done before the extensive North Korean provocations and belligerent rhetoric in 2022 and thus likely underrepresents current concerns about the North Korean threat (Dalton, Friedhoff, and Kim, 2022).

[10] The recent Korea Institute for National Unification poll by Lee et al. (2023, p. 27) asked about the likelihood of six serious risks (such as the risk of war) occurring if the ROK produces its own nuclear weapons, and all six were rated by respondents as serious.

weapon targets for North Korea. The citizens against having nuclear weapons in the ROK would likely pursue demonstrations against the nuclear weapons as against THAAD, although they would likely make those demonstrations far more serious and of greater magnitude. A future ROK president could simply cancel the ROK nuclear weapon program. Third, the cost of the ROK producing its own nuclear weapons would be very high. Production would take considerable time especially because the ROK lacks uranium enrichment and plutonium reprocessing capabilities. Fourth, to produce its own nuclear weapons, the ROK would need to leave the Nuclear Non-Proliferation Treaty. If it does so, the Nuclear Suppliers Group might refuse to provide the uranium needed for either ROK nuclear power plants or ROK nuclear weapons, potentially reducing or significantly eliminating perhaps 25 to 30 percent of ROK electrical power.[11] Fifth, the ROK could also suffer international economic sanctions that could be particularly devastating because of the ROK economy's emphasis on exports. Sixth, China would find it highly problematic that the ROK would create hundreds of nuclear weapons and might put substantial economic pressure on the ROK to not do so, including financial sanctions potentially much greater than those used against the THAAD deployment. And seventh, the United States could decide to withdraw from the ROK-U.S. military alliance. None of these potential outcomes is inevitable, but they are all quite possible. In trying to defend against the growing North Korean nuclear weapon threat, it is possible that the ROK could do serious damage to its security, economy, and reputation by pursuing this option.

The United States is strongly opposed to this option because the U.S. government is confident that its nuclear umbrella is adequate for deterring North Korea. Moreover, the United States still wishes to have a nuclear weapon–free Korean Peninsula (Byun, 2023), even though it is not currently the case (because of North Korean nuclear weapons) and is almost certainly an unrealistic objective.[12] In the 1970s, the United States threatened the ROK with alliance termination if it pursued its own nuclear weapons, and

---

[11] Nuclear energy provided 27.7 percent of ROK electricity in 2020 (U.S. Central Intelligence Agency, 2023).

[12] According to the definitive U.S. 2023 intelligence estimate, "Kim almost certainly views nuclear weapons and ICBMs as the ultimate guarantor of his autocratic rule and

that could happen again (Oberdorfer, 1997, pp. 68–73). These factors make this course of action a nonviable option.

Conditions could change dramatically if the United States elects a President who decides to withdraw the U.S. nuclear umbrella. The challenge that the ROK would then face would be the five or so years it would take to develop enough of its own nuclear weapons to stand up to North Korea, leaving the ROK with a window of vulnerability to the North. During that window, the North could potentially attack and destroy any ROK nuclear weapon production facilities that are developed, continuing the ROK vulnerability. Perhaps the only way for the ROK to manage such a challenge would be to insist on a (likely) secret agreement with the U.S. President that, in exchange for a ROK agreement to not develop its own nuclear weapons, the United States would agree to commit 50 to 100 nuclear weapons as an insurance package that would automatically transfer to the ROK if the United States decided to abandon the nuclear umbrella. Approximately 50 to 100 nuclear weapons would likely be sufficient for the ROK to manage the nuclear weapon production window of vulnerability with the North until it could indeed produce its own nuclear weapons. Of course, a new U.S. President could decide to abrogate such an agreement. But if the ROK had already paid to modernize those weapons, the new U.S. President would likely prefer to have a route to avoid becoming known as the U.S. leader who gave up the ROK to North Korean dominance.

Conclusions on the Future Nuclear Weapon Force Options

When dealing with the nuclear weapon threats of North Korea and China, the importance of strategic clarity will only increase in the future. The United States could prepare a plan for how to bring greater strategic clarity to its nuclear umbrella commitment to the ROK, similar to its agreements with NATO countries in the 1960s. The Washington Declaration could become such a plan if effectively implemented.

---

has no intention of abandoning those programs" (Office of the Director of National Intelligence, 2023).

With regard to nuclear weapon force commitments, the U.S. government might not be excited about any of the options. This conclusion emphasizes the importance of the ROK and United States reining in the North Korean nuclear weapon and CNM production. To achieve such an outcome, the ROK and United States must decide that they are willing to coerce North Korea and accept the risks of doing so. Otherwise, at some point, the United States could face a decision between allowing North Korean nuclear force superiority and creating an expanded tactical nuclear weapon force to support the ROK, the former being ill-advised. It almost certainly is not the case that the United States could simply avoid making a choice and rely on its strategic nuclear weapons to cover all nuclear force requirements in the ROK because the United States (1) no longer has many thousands of operational nuclear warheads, (2) has largely committed its strategic nuclear forces to dealing with Russia and China, and (3) faces a growing nuclear weapon threat from China that will increasingly push the United States into dedicating more of its strategic nuclear weapons to targets in China.

Thus, although both the ROK and U.S. governments would likely prefer to postpone any thinking about these alternatives for many years, the reality is that deciding how to handle the growing North Korean nuclear weapon threat and to provide ROK nuclear assurance would be best done in the short term. The United States could address these issues with a government study on the current and future security requirements of the ROK-U.S. alliance that recognizes the growing North Korean nuclear weapon threat. The United States does not want to be caught blind should the North decide that it has adequate nuclear forces to exercise coercive measures or offensive measures against the ROK or United States and can therefore carry out military attacks on the ROK with few negative consequences.[13] Such a condition could well press the ROK into producing nuclear weapons.

---

[13] If North Korean circumstances become increasingly unstable, which is possible, Kim might assume that his nuclear shadow will allow him to escalate his provocations to include limited attacks; such attacks could lead to dramatic ROK responses. A similar situation developed in 2010 when the ROK decided after the North Korean sinking of the *Cheonan* warship and shelling of the ROK Yeonpyeong Island to implement the ROK concept of proactive deterrence, which "called for commanders to take countermeasures three to five times stronger than an enemy attack" (Kim, 2014).

Nuclear Damage Assessment

Table 2.1 used a simple assessment of the potential lives lost and serious injuries resulting from North Korean nuclear weapon attacks against Seoul, New York City, and Beijing. This assessment was done by estimating the population density of each city and multiplying that by the estimated area in which fatalities and serious injuries would occur.[1] The area affected is based on information from the 1945 nuclear attack on Hiroshima. The nuclear weapon used in Hiroshima was detonated at a modest altitude, increasing prompt effects while eliminating most fallout, which is a choice we accept here. With nuclear effects, there are substantial complications and uncertainties in estimating effects. Because our objective is to demonstrate the order of magnitude of casualties caused rather than make a precise prediction, we work from best estimates of effects.

Population Density

We first calculate the population density of the three cities. For Seoul, we used data from City Population (undated-a). The city has a significant amount of low-population hill areas that an attacker would seek to avoid when trying to cause maximum casualties. We therefore selected three adjoining administrative districts with a higher population density: Dongdaemun Gu, Jungnang Gu, and Gwangjin Gu. In 2020, these districts had a

---

[1] Bruce W. Bennett had previously used the NukeMap program to make the kind of estimates shown in Table 2.1. Gregory S. Jones noted some apparent problems in the NukeMap calculations and suggested the methodology described herein as an alternative. Ultimately, the casualties are not substantially different.

combined population of 1,091,000 people, with a land area of 50 km², giving a population density of 21,900 people per km². For New York City, we used data from City Population (undated-b) and selected Manhattan as the target area; it had a population of 1,596,000 in 2022, with a land area of 58.7 km², giving a population density of 27,200 people per km². For Beijing, we used data from Demographia (undated), which lists the urban districts of Beijing; it had a population of 2,663,000 in 2000, with a land area of 87.1 per km², giving a population density of 30,600 people per square kilometer.

Note that each of these estimates is based on 50 to 90 km² of land area. The sixth North Korean nuclear test would have affected a larger land area, which would likely reach to locations with lower-density population. We therefore reduce the population density by 25 percent when calculating the number of people affected by the sixth nuclear test.

Note that the population data available tends to be for the residences of people. That density can shift dramatically during the workday. We have chosen to use the available data.

Lethal Area

The atomic bombing of Hiroshima provides the best source of data for the number of fatalities and injuries that might result from a nuclear attack. The Committee for the Compilation of Materials on Damage Caused by the Atomic Bombs in Hiroshima and Nagasaki (1981, p. 113) published data on the number of fatalities, serious injuries, and slight injuries contained in 0.5-km-radius rings around ground zero at Hiroshima. We focused on fatalities plus serious injuries.

For nuclear attacks on large urban areas, the data can be integrated to find an equivalent area, giving the same number of fatalities plus serious injuries that would be found by using a more complex approximation of the area. The integration can be done by a trapezoidal approximation. The equivalent area using the Committee for Compilation of Materials on Damage Caused by the Atomic Bombs in Hiroshima and Nagasaki (1981) data is 12.1 km². Toon et al. (2007, pp. 1978–1979) found that the curves from the committee can be well fitted by normal distributions. These curves can be easily integrated. Their equivalent fatalities plus injuries area is 13.3 km². We have averaged the two results and rounded to two places, which gives 13 km².

To scale the results to other yields, it is necessary to know the yield of the Hiroshima explosion. For many years, it was thought that the yield was 12.5 kt (Glasstone and Dolan, 1977, p. 36). However, as part of the effort to determine the long-term radiation effects from the Hiroshima bombings, Kerr et al. (2005, p. 54) reevaluated the yield. The current best estimate is 16 kt.

It is also hypothesized that, for weapons of 5 kt or larger, blast is the primary effect for which yield scaling of the affected area is needed. Normally, the area affected is scaled to the 0.67 power of yield compared with a base value, such as 16 kt. But doing so ignores the pulse duration of blast that causes blast effects to be even greater than the 0.67 power scaling for larger yield explosions. Using calculated effects areas for various yield weapons and curve fitting those values, we concluded that the inclusion of pulse duration causes the area affected to scale more with the 0.84 power of yield for weapons in the 5 kt to 250 kt range, which matches North Korea's second through sixth nuclear weapon tests. Thus, for North Korea's fifth nuclear test of about 18.8 kt, we estimate that the area for fatalities and serious injuries would be about 14.9 km², compared with 13 km² at 16 kt.

For weapon yields less than 5 kt, prompt radiation is the primary damage effect; it has a much lower scaling factor. Using curve fitting to existing serious casualty estimates, we estimate that the area affected by a 1.4 kt nuclear explosion would 2.9 km2.

Calculating Potential Fatalities and Serious Casualties

Both the population densities and the land areas affected are shown in Table A.1. Multiplying these two numbers by each other provides the estimates of fatalities and serious injuries shown in Table A.1 (and in Table 2.1). Note that these estimates are highly uncertain because of the uncertainties around the weapon yields and the differing population densities for different parts of the areas affected. These are thus very rough estimates.

TABLE A.1

Calculation of Potential Nuclear Weapon Effects

Test Number	Yield (kt)[a]	Land Area Affected (km²)	Fatalities and Serious Injuries[a]		
			Seoul (21,9000 people per km²)	Manhattan (27,200 people per km²)	Beijing (30,600 people per km²)
1	1.4	2.9	64,000	79,000	89,000
2	5.0	4.9	107,000	133,000	150,000
3	13.2	11.1	243,000	302,000	340,000
4	11.2	9.6	210,000	261,000	294,000
5	18.8	14.9	326,000	405,000	456,000
6	230.0	122.0	2,000,000	2,490,000	2,800,000

[a] Voytan et al., 2019.

Abbreviations

CCP	Chinese Communist Party
CFC	Combined Forces Command
CNM	critical nuclear material
CONOPS	concept of operations
COVID-19	coronavirus disease 2019
DCA	dual-capable aircraft
DIME	diplomatic, information, military, and economic
DoD	Department of Defense
DPRK	Democratic People's Republic of Korea
EDSCG	Extended Deterrence Strategy and Consultation Group
EMP	electromagnetic pulse
GMD	Ground-Based Midcourse Defense
ICBM	intercontinental ballistic missile
NCG	Nuclear Consultative Group
PLA	People's Liberation Army
PLARF	People's Liberation Army Rocket Force
PRC	People's Republic of China
ROK	Republic of Korea
START	Strategic Arms Reduction Treaty
THAAD	Terminal High Altitude Area Defense
TTX	tabletop exercise
UN	United Nations
WS3	weapons storage security system

Bibliography

Abrams, Robert B., "Statement of the Commander, United Nations Command; Commander, United States-Republic of Korea Combined Forces Command; and Commander, United States Forces Korea," testimony before the House Armed Services Committee, March 27, 2019.

Ahn, Jennifer, "The Evolution of South Korea's Nuclear Weapons Policy Debate," *Asia Unbound* blog, Council on Foreign Relations, August 16, 2022.

Albert, Eleanor, "The China–North Korea Relationship," Council on Foreign Relations, June 25, 2019.

Allard, Léonie, Mathieu Duchâtel, and François Godement, "Preempting Defeat: In Search of North Korea's Nuclear Doctrine," European Council on Foreign Relations, November 22, 2017.

Army Techniques Publication 7-100.2, *North Korean Tactics*, Department of the Army, July 24, 2020.

Asan Institute, "South Korea in a Changing World: Foreign Affairs," 2012.

Atwood, Kylie, and Jennifer Hansler, "Satellite Images Appear to Show China Is Making Significant Progress Developing Missile Silos That Could Eventually Launch Nuclear Weapons," CNN, November 2, 2021.

Baik Sung-won, "Leaked N. Korean Document Shows Internal Policy Against Denuclearization," *Voice of America*, June 17, 2019.

Bartlett, Jason, and Megan Ophel, "Sanctions by the Numbers: U.S. Secondary Sanctions," Center for New American Security, August 26, 2021.

Beauchamp-Mustafaga, Nathan, Derek Grossman, Kristen Gunness, Michael S. Chase, Marigold Black, and Natalia D. Simmons-Thomas, *Deciphering Chinese Deterrence Signalling in the New Era: An Analytic Framework and Seven Case Studies*, RAND Corporation, RR-A1074-1, 2021. As of August 18, 2023:
https://www.rand.org/pubs/research_reports/RRA1074-1.html

Bennett, Bruce W., *Assessing the Capabilities of Strategic Nuclear Forces: The Limits of Current Methods*, RAND Corporation, N-1441-NA, 1980a. As of August 18, 2023:
https://www.rand.org/pubs/notes/N1441.html

Bennett, Bruce W., *How to Assess the Survivability of U.S. ICBMs*, RAND Corporation, R-2577-FF, 1980b. As of August 18, 2023:
https://www.rand.org/pubs/reports/R2577.html

Bennett, Bruce W., *A Brief Analysis of the Republic of Korea's Defense Reform Plan*, RAND Corporation, OP-165-OSD, 2006. As of June 17, 2023: https://www.rand.org/pubs/occasional_papers/OP165.html

Bennett, Bruce W., *Preparing for the Possibility of a North Korean Collapse*, RAND Corporation, RR-331-SRF, 2013. As of August 18, 2023: https://www.rand.org/pubs/research_reports/RR331.html

Bennett, Bruce W., "South Korea: Capable Now, Questions for the Future," in Gary J. Schmitt, ed., *A Hard Look at Hard Power: Assessing the Defense Capabilities of Key U.S. Allies and Security Partners*, U.S. Army War College Strategic Studies Institute and U.S. Army War College Press, 2020.

Bennett, Bruce, "How to Stop North Korea's Missile Tests: One Million USB Drives Loaded with K-Pop?" *19FortyFive*, October 10, 2022a.

Bennett, Bruce W., "How Japan's Counterstrike Plans Help the ROK Defend Against North Korean Threats," NK News, December 27, 2022b.

Bennett, Bruce, "Why America Should Destroy North Korean ICBMs Fired into the Pacific Ocean," *19FortyFive*, March 13, 2023.

Bennett, Bruce W., Kang Choi, Myong-Hyun Go, Bruce E. Bechtol, Jr., Jiyoung Park, Bruce Klingner, and Du-Hyeogn Cha, *Countering the Risks of North Korean Nuclear Weapons*, RAND Corporation, PE-A1015-1, April 2021. As August 18, 2023: https://www.rand.org/pubs/perspectives/PEA1015-1.html

Bennett, Bruce W., Kang Choi, Gregory S. Jones, Du-Hyeogn Cha, Jiyoung Park, Scott W. Harold, Myong-Hyun Go, and Yun Kang, *Characterizing the Risks of North Korean Chemical and Biological Weapons, Electromagnetic Pulse, and Cyber Threats*, RAND Corporation, RR-A2026-1, 2022. As of August 18, 2023: https://www.rand.org/pubs/research_reports/RRA2026-1.html

Berlin Information-Center for Transatlantic Security, "NATO Nuclear Sharing and the NPT—Questions to Be Answered," June 1997.

Bermudez, Joseph S., "The Democratic People's Republic of Korea and Unconventional Weapons," in Peter R. Lavoy, Scott D. Sagan, James J. Wirtz, eds., *Planning the Unthinkable: How New Powers Will Use Nuclear, Biological, and Chemical Weapons*, Cornell University Press, 2000.

Bernstein, Richard, "Intelligence Has Its Limitations," *New York Times*, January 13, 2010.

Bosbotinis, James, "Hypersonic Defence 2022," Institute for Defense and Government Advancement, 2022.

Bowers, Ian, and Henrik Hiim, "South Korea, Conventional Capabilities, and the Future of the Korean Peninsula," *War on the Rocks*, February 11, 2021.

Bremer, Ifang, "Map Apps Add Locations Where South Koreans Can Shelter from North Korean Attack," NK News, July 4, 2023.

Brewer, Eric, and Toby Dalton, "South Korea's Nuclear Flirtations Highlight the Growing Risks of Allied Proliferation," Carnegie Endowment for International Peace, February 13, 2023.

Brewster, David, "Fighting a War in the Nuclear Shadow," Australian Strategic Policy Institute, March 10, 2022.

Bridley, Ryan, and Scott Pastor, "Military Drone Swarms and the Options to Combat Them," *Small Wars Journal*, August 19, 2022.

Brookings Institution, "Global Nuclear Stockpiles, 1945–1996," August 1998.

Burke, Edmund J., and Arthur Chan, "Coming to a (New) Theater Near You: Command, Control, and Forces," in Philip C. Saunders, Arthur S. Ding, Andrew Scobell, Andrew N. D. Yang, and Joel Wuthnow, eds., *Chairman Xi Remakes the PLA: Assessing Chinese Military Reforms*, National Defense University Press, 2019.

Byun Duk-kun, "U.S. Goal Remains 'Complete Denuclearization' of Korean Peninsula: State Dept.," Yonhap News Agency, March 28, 2023.

Center for Arms Control and Non-Proliferation, "U.S. Nuclear Weapons Modernization: Costs & Constraints," fact sheet, January 22, 2021a.

Center for Arms Control and Non-Proliferation, "U.S. Nuclear Weapons in Europe," fact sheet, August 18, 2021b.

Cha, Sangmi, "South Korea Asks U.S. for Greater Role in Managing Nuclear Weapons," Bloomberg, January 1. 2023.

Chae Yun-hwan, "S. Korea Approves Plans to Buy F-35A Fighters, SM-6 Interceptors," Yonhap News Agency, March 13, 2023.

Chan, Minnie, "High Hopes of China's H-20 Stealth Bomber Launch as PLA Top Brass Vow Weapon System Upgrades," *South China Morning Post*, November 11, 2022.

Cheong, Seong-Chang, "The Case for South Korea to Go Nuclear," *The Diplomat*, October 22, 2022.

CHEY Institute for Advanced Studies, "76% of the People 'Need Independent Nuclear Development' . . . 77% 'North Korea's Denuclearization Is Impossible,'" *Chosun Ilbo*, January 30, 2023.

Choe Sang-Hun, "Kim Jong-un Calls K-Pop a 'Vicious Cancer' in the New Culture War," *New York Times*, June 10, 2021.

Choe Sang-Hun, "North Korea Launches ICBM," *New York Times*, February 18, 2023.

Choi, David, "Trump Considered 'Complete Withdrawal' of U.S. Troops from South Korea, Former Defense Chief Says," *Stars and Stripes*, May 10, 2022a.

Choi, David, "North Korea's Proclamation on Preemptive Nuclear Strikes Was No Surprise, South Says," *Stars and Stripes*, September 13, 2022b.

Choi, David, "South Korea Prefers U.S. 'Strategic Assets' to Nuclear Weapons, Senior Official Says," *Stars and Stripes*, October 13, 2022c.

Choi, David, "South Korea to Expand Military Drills with Japan amid North Korean Threats, Defense Chief Says," *Stars and Stripes*, January 19, 2023.

Choi, Haejin, and Heekyong Yang, "South Korea Bomb Shelters Forgotten with No Food, Water as North Korea Threat Grows," Reuters, July 7, 2017.

Choi Kyung-woon, "S. Korea Nudges U.S. to Share Tactical Nukes," *Chosun Ilbo*, October 13, 2022.

Choi Kyung-woon and Kim Dong-ha, "There Is No Reason to Reject the Inter-Korean Summit, but It Is Not a Show," *Chosun Ilbo*, January 2, 2023.

Choi, S. Paul. "U.S.-ROK Alliance Consultative Mechanisms: Strengthening Deterrence, Providing Reassurance, Facing an Enduring Challenge," Korea Economic Institute, March 14, 2023.

Choy, Min Chao, "North Koreans Launder Money Through an Illegal Bank Account in Congo," NK News, August 20, 2020.

City Population, "SOUTH KOREA: Seoul Metropolitan City," webpage, undated-a. As of August 18, 2023:
http://citypopulation.de/en/southkorea/seoul/admin/

City Population, "USA: New York City Boroughs," webpage, undated-b. As of August 18, 2023:
http://www.citypopulation.de/en/usa/newyorkcity/

Committee for the Compilation of Materials on Damage Caused by the Atomic Bombs in Hiroshima and Nagasaki, *Hiroshima and Nagasaki: The Physical, Medical, and Social Effects of the Atomic Bombings*, trans. Eisei Ishikawa and David L. Swain, Basic Books Inc., 1981.

Congressional Budget Office, *Projected Costs of U.S. Nuclear Forces, 2021 to 2030*, May 24, 2021.

Costlow, Matthew, "Believe It or Not: U.S. Nuclear Declaratory Policy and Calculated Ambiguity," *War on the Rocks*, August 9, 2021.

Council on Foreign Relations, "North Korea's Military Capabilities," June 28, 2022.

Curtis E. Lemay Center, "Extended Deterrence," Air University, December 18, 2020.

Dalton, Toby, Karl Friedhoff, and Lami Kim, *Thinking Nuclear: South Korean Attitudes on Nuclear Weapons*, Chicago Council on Global Affairs, February 2022.

Defense Manpower Data Center, "Military and Civilian Personnel by Service/ Agency by State/Country," spreadsheet, September 2022.

Delory, Stéphane, Antoine Bondaz, and Christian Maire, "North Korean Short Range Systems: Military Consequences of the Development of the KN-23, KN-24 and KN-25," Hague Code of Conduct Against the Proliferation of Ballistic Missiles, Fondation pour la Recherche Stratégique, January 2023.

Demirjian, Karouri, "U.S. General Warns of China's Expanding Nuclear Arsenal," *Washington Post*, September 15, 2022.

Demographia "Beijing: Population & Density by District and County," webpage, undated. As of August 18, 2023:
http://demographia.com/db-beijing-ward.htm

Denyer, Simon, and Amanda Erickson, "Beijing Warns Pyongyang: You're on Your Own If You Go After the United States," *Washington Post*, August 11, 2017.

Dingman, Roger, "Atomic Diplomacy During the Korean War," *International Security*, Vol. 13, No. 3, Winter 1988–1989.

DoD—*See* U.S. Department of Defense.

Eberstadt, Nicholas, "A Skeptical View," *Wall Street Journal*, September 21, 2005.

Enthoven, Alain C., and K. V. Smith, *How Much Is Enough? Shaping the Defense Program, 1961–1969*, RAND Corporation, CB-403, 2005. As of August 18, 2023:
https://www.rand.org/pubs/commercial_books/CB403.html

Estes, Madison A., *Prevailing Under the Nuclear Shadow*, CNA, September 2020.

"Estimating North Korea's Nuclear Stockpiles: An Interview with Siegfried Hecker," *38 North*, April 30, 2021.

Feickert, Andrew, "The U.S. Army's Mid-Range Capability (MRC) Weapon System," Congressional Research Service, December 6, 2022.

Foot, Rosemary J., "Nuclear Coercion and the Ending of the Korean Conflict," *International Security*, Vol. 13, No. 3, Winter 1988–1989.

Fretwell, James, "Mad About THAAD: South Korea-China Dispute over U.S. Missile Interceptor Returns," NK News, July 28, 2022.

"Full Text of Washington Declaration Adopted at Yoon-Biden Summit," Yonhap News Agency, April 27, 2023.

Gallo, William, "Citing Trump, North Korea Defends Ballistic Missile Tests," *Voice of America*, August 10, 2019.

Gallo, William, "How the Afghanistan Withdrawal Looks from South Korea, America's Other 'Forever War,'" *Voice of America*, August 20, 2021.

Glasstone, Samuel, and Philip J. Dolan, *The Effects of Nuclear Weapons*, 3rd ed., U.S. Department of Defense and U.S. Department of Energy, 1977.

GlobalSecurity.org, "Korea Air and Missile Defense (KAMD)," webpage, undated. As of August 18, 2023:
https://www.globalsecurity.org/military/world/rok/kamd.htm

Go Myong-hyun, "North Korean Provocations and the Assurance Challenge for the ROK-U.S. Alliance," Asan Institute for Policy Studies, December 28, 2022.

Green, Christopher, "The 'Myth' of the Kill, Kill, Kill Chain," *Sino NK*, October 27, 2013.

Halloran, Richard, "Adding to the Rhetoric over North Korea: Talk of War," *New York Times*, December 7, 1998.

Hansen, M. V., "International Uranium Resources Evaluation Project: National Favourability Studies, Republic of Korea," International Atomic Energy Agency, December 1977.

Hecker, Siegfried, "The Disastrous Downsides of South Korea Building Nuclear Weapons," *38 North*, January 20, 2023.

Hecker, Siegfried S., Chaim Braun, and Chris Lawrence, "North Korea's Stockpiles of Fissile Material," *Korea Observer*, Vol. 47, No. 4, Winter 2016.

Heinonen, Olli, "North Korea's Nuclear Enrichment: Capabilities and Consequences," *38 North*, June 22, 2011.

Hersh, Seymour M., "The Cold Test: What the Administration Knew About Pakistan and the North Korean Nuclear Program," *New Yorker*, January 19, 2003.

Holcomb, M. Staser, "Modification of SSBN Commitments to NATO," Office of the Secretary of Defense, March 23, 1976.

Hsu, Spencer S., "Chinese Bank Involved in Probe on North Korean Sanctions and Money Laundering Faces Financial 'Death Penalty,'" *Washington Post*, June 24, 2019.

Hwang, Ildo, "Kim Jong Un Regime's Nuclear Missile Behavior and Kim Il Sung Memoir: A Strategic Culture Approach," *Korean Journal of Defense Analysis*, Vol. 34, No. 4, December 4, 2022.

Jelnov, Artyom, Yair Tauman, and Richard Zeckhauser, "Confronting an Enemy with Unknown Preferences: Deterrer or Provocateur?" *European Journal of Political Economy*, Vol. 54, September 2018.

Jeong Yong-Soo, Lee Chul-Jae, and Sarah Kim, "North Could Have 60 Nuclear Warheads," *JoongAng Ilbo*, February 9, 2017.

Jewell, Ethan, "40+ Launches, 174K Ethereum, 168* COVID Cases: North Korea's 2022 by the Numbers," NK News, December 30, 2022.

Ji Da-gyum, "U.S. Says It Supports Nuclear-Free Peninsula amid Dispute over Tactical Nuke Redeployment," *Korea Herald*, October 12, 2022.

Jones, Gregory S., "The Iraqi Ballistic Missile Program: The Gulf War and the Future of the Missile Threat," American Institute for Strategic Cooperation, Summer 1992.

Kajimoto, Tetsushi, and Takaya Yamaguchi, "Japan Unveils Record Budget in Boost to Defense Spending," Reuters, December 23, 2022.

Kang Byung-cheol, "U.S. Points to China as Sole Competitor Despite 'Russian Threat' . . . North Korea, Mentioned Three Times," Yonhap News Agency, August 13, 2022.

Karmanau, Yuras, Jim Heintz, Vladimir Isachenkov, and Dasha Litvinova, "Putin Puts Russia's Nuclear Forces on Alert, Escalating Tensions," Associated Press, February 27, 2022.

"KBS Reports Plan to Topple Kim Il-Sung," *Washington Times*, March 25, 1994.

Kerr, George D., Robert W. Young, Harry M. Cullings, and Robert F. Christy, "Bomb Parameters," in Robert W. Young and George D. Kerr, eds., *Reassessment of the Atomic Bomb Radiation Dosimetry for Hiroshima and Nagasaki: Dosimetry System 2002*, Vol. 1, Radiation Effects Research Foundation, 2005.

Kerr, Paul K., "China's Nuclear and Missile Proliferation," Congressional Research Service, February 1, 2023.

Kim, Cynthia, and Josh Smith, "North Korea Says Missile Tests Simulate Striking South with Nuclear Weapons," Reuters, October 9, 2022.

Kim Da-sol, "Lotte Seeks to Exit China After Investing $7.2b," *Korea Herald*, March 13, 2019.

Kim Eun-jung, "S. Korea Responds to North's Artillery with New Engagement Rules," Yonhap News Agency, April 1, 2014.

Kim Hwan Yong, "U.S. Ambassador to South Korea, Goldberg, 'Firm Will to Extended Deterrence' . . . Negative Stance on 'Redeployment of Tactical Nuclear Weapons in Korea,'" *Voice of America*, August 18, 2022.

Kim, J. James, Kang Chungku, and Ham Geon Hee, "South Korean Public Opinion on ROK-U.S. Bilateral Ties," Asan Institute for Policy Studies, May 2022.

Kim, Jeongmin, "Full Text: How North Korea Transformed Its Nuclear Doctrine Law," NK News, September 9, 2022.

Kim, Jeongmin, "Full Text: Yoon Suk-yeol's Remarks on South Korea Acquiring Nuclear Arms," NK News, January 13, 2023.

Kim Ji-hyun, "Uproar over Seoul's Attempt to Change Nuke Umbrella Term," *Korea Herald*, October 20, 2006.

Kim Minseok and Chen Chuanren, "South Korea Unveils 'Bunker Buster' as North Ramps Up Missiles Tests," Aviation Week Intelligence Network, October 4, 2022.

Kim, Sarah, "U.S. Affirms Nuclear Umbrella over South Korea," *Joongang Ilbo*, November 30, 2021.

Kim Soo-yeon and Chae Yun-hwan, "(5th LD) N. Korea's Missile Flies Across NLL for 1st Time; S. Korea Sends Missiles Northward in Its Show of Force," Yonhap News Agency, November 2, 2022.

Kim Tong-Hyung, "North Korea Says It Will Never Give Up Nukes to Counter U.S.," *AP News*, September 8, 2022.

Kirkpatrick, Melanie, "To Disarm North Korea, Focus on Human Rights," *Wall Street Journal*, March 5, 2023.

Korean Immigration Service, *Yearbook of Korea Immigration Statistics 2021*, 2022.

"Koreans Distrust Chinese More Than Russians, Japanese," *JoongAng Ilbo*, August 24, 2022.

Kort, Ryan W., Carlos R. Bersabe, Dalton H. Clarke, and Derek J. Di Bello, "Twenty-First Century Nuclear Deterrence: Operationalizing the 2018 Nuclear Posture Review," *Joint Force Quarterly*, Vol. 94, 3rd quarter, 2019.

Kraterou, Alike, and Jack Evans, "China Warns of World War III with 'Nuclear Sword Hanging over Our Heads' over Putin's Plan to Send Nukes to Belarus," news.com.au, April 2, 2023.

Kristensen, Hans M., "U.S. Nuclear Weapons in Europe: A Review of Post-Cold War Policy, Force Levels, and War Planning," Natural Resources Defense Council, February 2005a.

Kristensen, Hans M., "A History of U.S. Nuclear Weapons in South Korea," Nuclear Information Project, September 28, 2005b.

Kristensen, Hans, "NATO Steadfast Noon Exercise and Nuclear Modernization in Europe," Federation of American Scientists, October 17, 2022.

Kristensen, Hans M., and Matt Korda, "Nuclear Notebook: United States Nuclear Weapons, 2021," *Bulletin of the Atomic Scientists*, Vol. 77, No. 1, January 2021a.

Kristensen, Hans M., and Matt Korda, "North Korean Nuclear Weapons, 2021," *Bulletin of the Atomic Scientists*, Vol. 77, No. 4, July 2021b.

Kristensen, Hans M., and Matt Korda, "Russian Nuclear Weapons, 2022," *Bulletin of the Atomic Scientists*, Vol. 78, No. 2, March 2022a.

Kristensen, Hans M., and Matt Korda, "United States Nuclear Weapons, 2022," *Bulletin of the Atomic Scientists*, Vol. 78, No. 3, May 2022b.

Kristensen, Hans M., and Robert S. Norris, "Global Nuclear Weapons Inventories, 1945–2013," *Bulletin of the Atomic Scientists*, Vol. 69, No. 5, September–October 2013.

Kristensen, Hans M., and Robert S. Norris, "A History of U.S. Nuclear Weapons in South Korea," *Bulletin of the Atomic Scientists*, Vol. 73, No. 6, November 2017.

Landay, Jonathan, and Arshad Mohammed, "U.S. to Stop Giving Russia Some New START Nuclear Arms Data," Reuters, June 1, 2023.

Lankov, Andrei, "In Washington, Worries of ROK Nukes Steal Spotlight from North Korean Missiles," NK News, June 5, 2023.

"Leaders from Japan and South Korea Vow Better Ties Following Summit," NPR, May 8, 2023.

Lee Chae Un, "Many North Koreans React to Test Launch of Hwasong-17 with Criticism," *Daily NK*, April 4, 2022.

Lee, Christy, "Experts: South Korea Seeks Enhanced U.S. Nuclear Assurances Against North Korea," *Voice of America*, January 18, 2023.

Lee Haye-ah, "S. Korea Grapples with Calls for Nuclear Armament," Yonhap News Agency, October 13, 2022.

Lee Haye-ah, "Yoon Says S. Korea, U.S. in Talks over Joint Nuclear Exercises," Yonhap News Agency, January 2, 2023a.

Lee Haye-ah, "Yoon Announces 'Complete Normalization' of Military Intel-Sharing Pact with Japan Diplomacy," Yonhap News Agency, March 16, 2023b.

Lee Haye-ah, "Yoon Vows to Build Strong Security Through 'Peace by Overwhelming Power,'" Yonhap News Agency, May 2, 2023c.

Lee Jong-seop, "54th SCM, ROK-U.S. Alliance and Strengthening Execution of Extended Deterrence [Contributed by the Minister of Defense]," *Dong-a Ilbo* November 7, 2022.

Lee, Michelle Ye Hee, "South Koreans Overwhelmingly Want Nuclear Weapons to Confront China and North Korea, Poll Finds," *Washington Post*, January 21, 2022.

Lee, Michelle Ye Hee, and Min Joo Kim, "South Korea Clings to North's Denuclearization, Despite Dwindling Chances," *Washington Post*, November 26, 2022.

Lee, Sang Sin, Tae-eun Min, Kwang-il Yoon, Bon-sang Koo, and Peter Gries, "KINU Unification Survey 2020," press briefing, Korea Institute of National Unification, June 26, 2020.

Lee, Sang Sin, Tae-eun Min, Kwang-il Yoon, and Bon-sang Koo, *KINU Unification Survey 2023: Public Opinion on South Korea's Nuclear Armament*, Korea Institute of National Unification, June 2023.

Lee, Sang Yong, "North Korea's War Against Outside Information and Culture," *38 North*, May 25, 2023.

Lee Tae-hoon, "Defense Chief Tells Troops to Act First, Report Later," *Korea Times*, March 1, 2011.

Lendon, Brad, and Gawon Bae, "Kim Jong Un Calls for Exponential Increase in North Korea's Nuclear Arsenal amid Threats from South, U.S.," CNN, January 2, 2023.

Lewis, Jeffrey, "It's Time to Accept That North Korea Has Nuclear Weapons," *New York Times*, October 13, 2022.

Logan, David C., "Making Sense of China's Missile Forces," in Philip C. Saunders, Arthur S. Ding, Andrew Scobell, Andrew N. D. Yang, and Joel Wuthnow, eds., *Chairman Xi Remakes the PLA: Assessing Chinese Military Reforms*, National Defense University Press, 2019.

Losey, Stephen, "You Can Call 2007 Nuke Mishandling an Embarrassment, but Don't Call It the 'Minot Incident,'" *Air Force Times*, June 25, 2019.

Mann, Jim, "Scenarios for a 2nd Korean War Grim for U.S., South," *Los Angeles Times*, February 22, 1994.

Mazarr, Michael J., Arthur Chan, Alyssa Demus, Bryan Frederick, Alireza Nader, Stephanie Pezard, Julia A. Thompson, and Elina Treyger, *What Deters and Why: Exploring Requirements for Effective Deterrence of Interstate Aggression*, RAND Corporation, RR-2451-A, 2018. As of April 17, 2023: https://www.rand.org/pubs/research_reports/RR2451.html

McCall, Stephen M., and Kelly M. Sayler, "Defense Primer: Ballistic Missile Defense," Congressional Research Service, November 23, 2022.

McNamara, Robert, "Statement Made on Saturday 5 May by Secretary McNamara at the NATO Ministerial Meeting in Athens," North Atlantic Council, May 5, 1962.

Meick, Ethan, and Nargiza Salidjanova, *China's Response to U.S.-South Korean Missile Defense System Deployment and Its Implications*, U.S.-China Economic and Security Review Commission, July 26, 2017.

Missile Defense Advocacy Alliance, "Republic of Korea," December 2022.

Missile Defense Project, "Hwasong-7 (Nodong 1)," Center for Strategic and International Studies, August 9, 2016, last updated July 31, 2021a.

Missile Defense Project, "Hyunmoo-2C," Center for Strategic and International Studies, July 31, 2021b.

Missile Defense Project, "JL-2," Center for Strategic and International Studies, August 12, 2016, last updated July 31, 2021c.

Moon Sung-hwi, "North Korea Moves Its Wartime Command Center to Nampo Taesan," *Liberty Korea Post*, July 7, 2018.

Mun Dong Hui, "North Koreans Struggle to Prepare for the Frigid Winter Weather," *Daily NK*, December 16, 2022.

Mutual Defense Treaty Between the United States and the Republic of Korea, signed at Washington, D.C., October 1, 1953.

Myers, Diana Y., *Thinking About the Unthinkable: Examining North Korea's Military Threat to China*, dissertation, RAND Pardee Graduate School, RAND Corporation, RGSD-A2469-1, 2022. As of August 18, 2023: https://www.rand.org/pubs/rgs_dissertations/RGSDA2469-1.html

Nam Hyun-woo, "Yoon Urges Xi to 'Play Active Role' in Reining in North Korea," *Korea Times*, November 15, 2022.

Nam Kyung-don, "S. Koreans Grow More Skeptical of NK's Denuclearization: Survey," *Korea Herald*, September 27, 2022.

National Intelligence Council, "North Korea: Scenarios for Leveraging Nuclear Weapons Through 2030," January 2023.

National Research Council of the National Academies, *Effects of Nuclear Earth-Penetrator and Other Weapons*, National Academies Press, 2005.

NATO—*See* North Atlantic Treaty Organization.

"NATO Begins Nuclear Exercises amid Russia War Tensions," Associated Press, October 17, 2022.

Norris, Robert S., and Hans M. Kristensen, "U.S. Nuclear Weapons in Europe, 1954–2004," *Bulletin of the Atomic Scientists*, Vol. 60, No. 6, November–December 2004.

North Atlantic Treaty Organization, "NATO's Nuclear Sharing Arrangements," fact sheet, February 2022a.

North Atlantic Treaty Organization, "Nuclear Planning Group (NPG)," May 9, 2022b.

"North Korea's Nuclear Programme Going 'Full Steam Ahead,' IAEA Chief Says," Reuters, September 20, 2021.

Nuclear Threat Initiative, "North Korea: Nuclear Overview," fact sheet, October 11, 2018.

Nuclear Threat Initiative, "North Korea Missile Overview," fact sheet, December 16, 2020.

Nuclear Weapon Archive, "Complete List of All U.S. Nuclear Weapons," webpage, last updated March 30, 2023. As of August 18, 2023: https://nuclearweaponarchive.org/Usa/Weapons/Allbombs.html

Oberdorfer, Don, "U.S. Decides to Withdraw A-Weapons from S. Korea," *Washington Post*, October 19, 1991.

Oberdorfer, Don, *The Two Koreas: A Contemporary History*, Addison-Wesley, 1997.

O'Carroll, Chad, "North Korea's First-Use Nuclear Doctrine: Key Drivers and Implications," NK News, September 9, 2022.

O'Carroll, Chad, and Chaewon Chung, "South Korean Media Consumption Top Reason for Execution in North Korea: Report," NK News, December 15, 2021.

O'Connor, Tom, "Trump Says He Likes North Korea's Kim, Calls South Korea President Moon 'Weak,'" *Newsweek*, April 23, 2021.

Office of the Director of National Intelligence, *Annual Threat Assessment of the U.S. Intelligence Community*, February 6, 2023.

O'Rourke, Ronald, "Navy Columbia (SSBN-826) Class Ballistic Missile Submarine Program: Background and Issues for Congress," Congressional Research Service, updated December 21, 2022.

Panda, Ankit, "China and North Korea Have a Mutual Defense Treaty, but When Would It Apply?" *The Diplomat*, August 14, 2017.

Panda, Ankit, "South Korea's 'Decapitation' Strategy Against North Korea Has More Risks Than Benefits," Carnegie Endowment for International Peace, August 15, 2022.

Panda, Ankit, "North Korea Places Tactical Nukes Front and Center with New Year's Day Launch," NK News, January 1, 2023.

Park Bo-ram, "S. Korea Unveils Plan to Raze Pyongyang in Case of Signs of Nuclear Attack," Yonhap News Agency, September 9, 2016.

Park, Hwee-Rhak, "What Should the United States Do to Dissuade South Koreans from Developing Nuclear Weapons?" Hansun Foundation, February 7, 2023.

Park Si-soo, "South Korea Hires SpaceX to Launch Five Spy Satellites by 2025," *Space News*, April 11, 2022.

Park Won Gon, "Strategic Implications of the USFK Relocation to Pyeongtaek," Korea Institute for Defense Analyses, No. 164, October 20, 2017.

Pearson, James, and Rozanna Latiff, "North Korean Spy Agency Runs Arms Operation Out of Malaysia, U.N. Says," Reuters, February 26, 2107.

Peng Guangqian and Yao Youzhi, eds., *The Science of Military Strategy*, Military Science Publishing House, Academy of Military Science of the Chinese People's Liberation Army, 2005.

Ponnudurai, Parameswaran, "Global Bid to Cripple North Korea's Illicit Trade," Radio Free Asia, March 5, 2013.

Reddy, Shreyas, "US-ROK Nuclear Coordination Group 'More Effective' Than NATO Analog: Yoon," NK News, May 2, 2023a.

Reddy, Shreyas, "Cybercrime Funds Half of North Korea's Missile Program, U.S. Official Says," NK News, May 11, 2023b.

Rengifo-Keller, Lucas, "Food Insecurity in North Korea Is at Its Worst Since the 1990s Famine," *38 North*, January 19, 2023.

Republic of Korea, Constitution of the Republic of Korea, official consolidated translation, July 12, 1948, amended October 29, 1987.

RFA Korean, "North Korea's Kim Jong Un Vows to Never Give Up Nuclear Weapons," Radio Free Asia, September 9, 2022.

Roberts, Brad, *Living with a Nuclear-Arming North Korea: Deterrence Decisions in a Deteriorating Threat Environment*, Stimson Center, November 4, 2020.

ROK—*See* Republic of Korea.

Roth, Andrew, "Russia Moving Nuclear Warheads to Belarus, Says Country's Leader," *The Guardian*, May 25, 2023.

Savkov, Nikita "Chinese Views of the United States amid Rising Sino-American Clashes," *China Brief*, Vol. 20, No. 11, June 24, 2020.

Schelling, Thomas C., "The Future of Arms Control," *Operations Research*, Vol. 9, No. 5, September–October 1961.

Schwartz, Thomas A., "Statement of the Commander in Chief United Command/Combined Forces Command & Commander, United States Forces Korea," testimony before the U.S. Senate Armed Services Committee, March 5, 2002.

The Science of Second Artillery Campaigns, PLA Publishing House, 2003.

Scobell, Andrew, Edmund J. Burke, Cortez A. Cooper III, Sale Lilly, Chad J. R. Ohlandt, Eric Warner, and J.D. Williams, *China's Grand Strategy: Trends, Trajectories, and Long-Term Competition*, RAND Corporation, RR-2798-A, 2020. As of August 18, 2023: https://www.rand.org/pubs/research_reports/RR2798.html

"Senior Politician Calls for S. Korea to Have Nuclear Weapons," Yonhap News Agency, January 31, 2016.

Shanker, Thom, "Missile Parts Sent to Taiwan in Error," *New York Times*, March 26, 2008.

Shim, Elizabeth, "South Korea Confirms It Has Military Plan to Remove Kim Jong Un," United Press International, September 21, 2016.

Shin, Hyonhee, "North Korea's Kim Orders More Production of Weapons-Grade Nuclear Materials," Reuters, March 27, 2023a.

Shin, Hyonhee, "N. Korea Says U.S.-S.Korea Drills Push Tension to 'Brink of Nuclear War,'" Reuters, April 6, 2023b.

Shou Xiaosong, *Science of Military Strategy*, 3rd ed., Academy of Military Science Press, 2013.

Smith, David, "Barack Obama at Nuclear Summit: 'Madmen' Threaten Global Security," *The Guardian*, April 1, 2016.

Smith, Josh, "Analysis: S.Korea Blazes New Path with 'Most Potent' Conventional Missile Submarine," Reuters, September 8, 2021.

Smith, R. Jeffrey, and Joby Warrick, "Pakistani Scientist Depicts More Advanced Nuclear Program in North Korea," *Washington Post*, December 28, 2009.

Song Sang-ho, "Military Under Fire Over Reactions," *Korea Herald*, November 24, 2010.

Song Sang-ho, "S. Korea's Vice Defense Minister Briefed on Key U.S. Strategic Assets During Visit to Local Base," Yonhap News Agency, September 16, 2022a.

Song Sang-ho, "S. Korea, U.S. Codify 4 Categories of 'Extended Deterrence' Cooperation Against N.K. Nuke Threats," Yonhap News Agency, November 4, 2022b.

Song Sang-ho, "NK Drones-Security Challenge," Yonhap News Agency, December 27, 2022c.

Song Sang-ho and Chae Yun-hwan, "S. Korea's Military to Introduce 'Kill Web' Concept to Counter N. Korea's Missile, Nuke Threats," Yonhap News Agency, March 3, 2023.

Stokes, Mark A., *China's Nuclear Warhead Storage and Handling System*, Project 2049 Institute, March 12, 2010.

Szalontai, Balazs, and Sergey Radchenko, "North Korea's Efforts to Acquire Nuclear Technology and Nuclear Weapons: Evidence from Russian and Hungarian Archives," working paper, Woodrow Wilson International Center for Scholars, August 2006.

Takemoto, Yoshifumi, and Kaori Kaneko, "Japan, South Korea to Link Radar Systems to Track N. Korea Missiles—Source," Reuters, May 9, 2023.

Taylor, Adam, "The Forgotten Story of Tens of Thousands of Koreans Who Died in Hiroshima," *Washington Post*, May 25, 2016.

Thielmann, Greg, "The Missile Gap Myth and Its Progeny," *Arms Control Today*, Vol. 41, No. 4, May 2011.

Toon, O. B, R. P. Turco, A. Robock, C. Bardeen, L. Oman, and G. L. Stenchikov, "Atmospheric Effects and Societal Consequences of Regional Scale Nuclear Conflicts and Acts of Individual Nuclear Terrorism," *Atmospheric Chemistry and Physics*, Vol. 7, 2007.

Treaty of Co-operation, Friendship, and Mutual Assistance Between the People's Republic of China and Democratic People's Republic Korea, signed at Beijing, July 11, 1961.

Treaty on the Non-Proliferation of Nuclear Weapons, January 7, 1968.

"Ukraine Conflict Update—Feb 27, 2022," SOF News, February 27, 2022.

"US Accuses Russia, China of Covering for North Korea at UN," *Voice of America*, August 25, 2023.

U.S. Central Intelligence Agency, "North Korea," in *The World Factbook*, updated March 22, 2023.

U.S. Department of Defense, *Nuclear Posture Review [Excerpts]*, January 2002.

U.S. Department of Defense, *Deterrence Operations: Joint Operating Concept*, version 2, December 2006.

U.S. Department of Defense, *Report on Nuclear Employment Strategy of the United States*, 2013.

U.S. Department of Defense, *2018 Nuclear Posture Review Report*, February 2018.

U.S. Department of Defense, *DoD Dictionary of Military and Associated Terms*, November 2021.

U.S. Department of Defense, "Joint Statement on the Extended Deterrence Strategy and Consultation Group Meeting," press release, September 16, 2022a.

U.S. Department of Defense, *2022 Nuclear Posture Review Report*, October 27, 2022b.

U.S. Department of Defense, "Missile Defense Agency Officials Hold a Press Briefing on President Biden's Fiscal 2024 Missile Defense Budget," March 14, 2023a.

U.S. Department of Defense, "Joint Press Release: Extended Deterrence Strategy and Consultation Group," press release, September 15, 2023.

U.S. Department of State, "New Start Treaty," undated.

U.S. Department of State, Office of the Historian, "Memorandum of Conversation," *Foreign Relations of the United States, 1961–1963*, Vol. XIV, *Berlin Crisis, 1961–1962*, May 31, 1961. As of September 19, 2023: https://history.state.gov/historicaldocuments/frus1961-63v14/d3

U.S. Department of the Treasury, "Treasury Sanctions Individual, Banks, and Trading Company for Supporting North Korea's WMD and Ballistic Missile Programs," press release, May 27, 2022.

"U.S. Eyes New Framework on Nuclear Deterrence with Japan, South Korea," *Kyodo News*, March 9, 2023.

U.S. Marine Corps Intelligence Activity, *North Korea Country Handbook*, U.S. Department of Defense, May 1997.

U.S. Office of the Secretary of Defense, *Military and Security Developments Involving the People's Republic of China, 2021*, U.S. Department of Defense, 2021.

U.S. Office of the Secretary of Defense, *Military and Security Developments Involving the People's Republic of China, 2022*, U.S. Department of Defense, November 29, 2022.

Voytan, Dimitri P., Thorne Lay, Esteban Chaves, and John T. Ohman, "Yield Estimates for the Six North Korean Nuclear Tests From Teleseismic P Wave Modeling and Intercorrelation of P and Pn Recordings," *Journal of Geophysical Research: Solid Earth*, Vol. 124, No. 5, May 2019.

Vu, Khang, "Why China and North Korea Decided to Renew a 60-Year-Old Treaty," *The Interpreter*, July 30, 2021.

Wampler, Robert A., *NATO Strategic Planning and Nuclear Weapons, 1950–1957*, Center for International Security Studies, Maryland School of Public Affairs, University of Maryland, January 1, 1990.

White House, "Joint Vision for the Alliance of the United States of America and the Republic of Korea," press release, June 16, 2009.

White House, "Phnom Penh Statement on US-Japan-Republic of Korea Trilateral Partnership for the Indo-Pacific," November 13, 2022.

White House, "The Spirit of Camp David: Joint Statement of Japan, the Republic of Korea, and the United States," August 18, 2023.

Work, Clint, "How, Exactly, Can the U.S. Strengthen Extended Deterrence?" *The Diplomat*, November 8, 2022.

Xiao Tianliang, ed., *The Science of Military Strategy*, National Defense University Press, 2020.

Yang, Uk, "Is South Korea Going Nuclear?" *38 North*, February 3, 2023.

Yoon, Sukjoon, "Upgrading South Korean THAAD," *The Diplomat*, May 10, 2021.

Yost, David S., "Assurance and U.S. Extended Deterrence in NATO," *International Affairs*, Vol. 85, No. 4, July 2009.

Zhou Peng and Yun Enbing, "Developing the Theory of Strategic Deterrence with Chinese Characteristics," *China Military Science*, Vol. 3, No. 20, 2004.

Zwirko, Colin, "North Korea's Recent Missile Tests Are Nuclear Warning to U.S., ROK: State Media," NK News, October 10, 2022.

Zwirko, Colin, "Kim Jong Un Vows to 'Exponentially' Increase Nuke Production to Counter U.S., ROK," NK News, January 1, 2023a.

Zwirko, Colin, "North Korea Says It Tested 'Strategic Cruise Missiles' from Submarine," NK News, March 13, 2023b.